POWER
FOR GOOD

POWER

FOR GOOD

Saying "Yes!" to life's invitations...

DAVID J SERLIN

A record of this publication is available from the British Library.

ISBN 978-1-910027-31-8

Typesetting by Wordzworth Ltd
www.wordzworth.com

Cover design by Titanium Design Ltd
www.titaniumdesign.co.uk

Cover image with gratitude to Naian Wang
www.images.unsplash.com

Published by Local Legend
www.local-legend.co.uk

**LOCAL
LEGEND**

"There is a Power for Good in the universe that is greater than we are, that we can use!"

ERNEST HOLMES

To my darling wife Lin,
my companion, confidante
and constant source of inspiration.

Acknowledgements

With deep gratitude to my dear parents, passed on to the Light,
to Gordon, Glyn and Judith, Dr Mark, Dr Roger and Kathy Juline,
to Dr Kathy Hearn and Dr Roger Teel, to Reverend Anya
and 'the teachings' for the highest good of all.

www.local-legend.co.uk

About the Author

David J Serlin was born in Stanmore, Middlesex, and now lives in Hertfordshire, UK, with his wife Linda and their son.

Always intrigued by the mysteries of the universe and of time and space, David was an avid reader of science fiction and subsequently the new breed of spiritual classics. This led him, following a successful career in sales, marketing and property management, to train as a spiritual healer (NFSH), a Positive Thinking practitioner (Peiffer Foundation) and a licensed practitioner of New Thought / Science of Mind (RScp).

Embarking on a spiritual journey together, David and Linda shared quite remarkable experiences, many of which are described here. As a result they have founded their own Spiritual Living group and now work together as a team, each contributing their unique talents and expertise, offering workshops and one-to-one sessions in all aspects of spiritual development.

They show how to apply universal spiritual principles in dealing with life's everyday challenges. Above all, they believe in making spirituality relevant, accessible to all – and fun!

"I hope," David says, "that this book will inspire others on their own, unique spiritual journeys and discover for themselves the universal Power for Good that is available to us all."

www.newthoughtnewyou.co.uk

Previous Publications

HIGHWAY TO HEALING (TUDOR PRESS, 1992)

ISBN 1 874514 01 1

The remarkable yet true story of how the author's father, Leonard Serlin, became a healer.

About This Book

The path to enlightenment is never easy. It takes courage,
determination, commitment – and an open mind!

Life is full of 'invitations', opportunities for growth and change, for adventure and discovery, if we heed the signs, follow the cues and keep our eyes open. Yet paramount amongst spiritual laws is that we always have free will: we always have a choice whether to accept or refuse the many invitations that may come our way.

My wife and I said "Yes!" to Spirit's subtle urgings and this book is the story of how that choice changed our lives and set us on an exciting journey of discovery and revelation. From a stately home near Stansted in Essex, UK, to an esoteric retreat on the north Californian coast of America, our path interweaves empowering spiritual insights and principles with landmark events and experiences. From the mystique of Spiritualism to the profound wisdom of New Thought and the Science of Mind, our experiences have enriched our souls, enlightened our minds, uplifted our spirits – and continue to do so.

Saying "Yes" to life's invitations, accepting challenge and being prepared to move beyond our comfort zones, can transform our lives and provide opportunities to move from the ordinary to the extraordinary, from stressed to blessed, to discover and fulfil our true potential.

This book offers practical spiritual tools, principles and processes to help us deal more effectively with life's issues and to harness and use the Power for Good in the universe that is greater than we are.

Truth, like beauty, is in the eyes of the beholder.
Learn from others' experience, be inspired by their success,
but only accept that which makes sense for you.

Contents

The room was silent and dark save for the soft, low light of a solitary lamp that cast an eerie, shadowy glow. We sat among strangers, a light tension of expectation hovering around each one.

Then it began...

A voice echoed from an empty corner of the room, faint at first like a whisper, straining for breath and almost choking with emotion. Gradually it gained strength.

"Lily... It's... John... It's me..."

An elderly lady in the audience cried out in startled recognition and joy.

"John! Is that really you?" Her tears of relief and love flowed.

And then there was silence again as a misty cloud of white substance, ectoplasm, swirled and shrouded the sleeping medium. We could barely believe what we had just experienced. But this was no dream.

It Started with a 'Phone Call

A dazzling golden orb of brilliant light illuminated the faces of the four figures sitting round a large, glistening white marble table. Hunched over and deep in conversation, they were clearly discussing something of great importance. Then one of the figures stood up and beckoned to another standing some way in the distance. He spoke in a soft, mellow tone, choosing his words carefully.

"It is time to leave," he said, barely concealing the sadness in his voice. "Your mission is set, there can be no turning back." Then his tone lifted as if he had recognised the underlying joy of the event. "You will be embarking on an amazing adventure, during which you will experience the many facets of Spirit. You will receive enlightened thoughts – the principles. We only ask that you live your life according to 'the Law' and share your understanding with all who will listen…" Then he paused again as if waiting for instruction or pondering a further thought.

"One other thing… You will have free will to accept or refuse the many invitations that may come your way. We will always be there to

1

guide and inspire you, if you so choose, but we cannot – and will not – try to influence your path or lead you one way or another."

I was listening intently but a strange, magnetic feeling seemed to be pulling me away from these, my teachers and friends. I tried to resist but the four figures quickly faded, and I knew that I would be leaving the presence of the Enlightened Ones for a while. A vaporous mist engulfed the scene and they disappeared, ghost-like, leaving me alone.

In the far distance, I heard the faint words, "By the way, you will soon forget all about this."

Then the alarm clock rang with an unfriendly shrillness and I awoke with a start.

"Wow, that *was* some strange dream!"

I cleared my head, stretched my arms, yawned and got out of bed, drew back the curtains and contemplated the day ahead. The morning sun poured in, promising a good one. After breakfast, the `phone rang. It was my girlfriend, Linda. We were both really into yoga at the time and had been looking for an interesting course or retreat to do together. She seemed excited.

"Look, I had to call you. I've just heard about this amazing place near Stansted where they run yoga courses. What do you think?"

"Sounds great," I responded, not really listening to her every word as she was prone to over-exuberance, but I went along with it. "Check out the dates and let me know." An hour later the `phone rang again.

"Sorry," she apologised, "I must have got it wrong. I called Stansted Hall and they no longer run yoga courses there but…" I waited. "They invited us to join one of their Spiritual Awareness Weeks. Shall we go?"

She sounded so enthusiastic I couldn't let her down, though I had no idea what she was talking about or what we were letting ourselves in for. Then I was stirred by some strange and sudden impulse.

"Yes, sure," I found myself saying, "let's go for it."

And that was it, the first of many 'invitations' we both felt impelled to accept. Thank heavens we did, as it was to open the door to many amazing new experiences and lead us both into a whole new world of incredible possibilities.

We had never even heard of Stansted Hall, let alone contemplated spending a week there, but something in their advertisement really captured our imagination.

Discover your true potential.
Psychic & Spiritual Awareness Week
at the Arthur Findlay College, Stansted Hall.

On a bright and sunny spring day with the scent of blossom in the air, we packed our bags and maps (pre-satnav) and headed north from our home in London through the winding country lanes and picturesque villages of Hertfordshire until we came to the historic town of Stansted Mountfitchet. The journey, taking the scenic route, took us a leisurely couple of hours but when we arrived it was like going back in time. Driving slowly up the narrow gravel driveway that led to the Hall, we both felt a frisson of excitement and a real sense of anticipation as we wondered what on Earth we had let ourselves in for...

Having parked the car we carried our cases up the grey stone steps leading to the entrance of the imposing Victorian mansion and paused for a moment to ring the bell. The heavy oak doors creaked open and we stepped into the wood-panelled lobby to a blazing open fire and a warm and welcoming reception that quickly dispelled any lingering doubts or reservations we may have had.

It was not just stepping back in time – it was like stepping into a whole new world. There were portraits on the walls of famous spiritualists from the past, including Arthur Findlay himself, the previous owner of the house who had bequeathed his home and entire estate in the 1960s to the Spiritualists' National Union 'for the advancement of Spiritualism and psychic science'. Now just minutes from Stansted airport and within earshot of the busy M11 motorway, the Hall seems to have survived as an oasis of peace and tranquillity, a sanctuary for all who seek to deepen their knowledge and understanding of Spirit.

We checked in and placed ourselves and our cases in the tiny, rickety old Victorian lift that clattered unceremoniously up to the first floor where we made our way down a dimly lit corridor to our room for the week. Our bedroom was a pleasant surprise – we must have landed 'the honeymoon suite' – being grand and spacious with large sash windows and a prestigious four-poster bed replete with faded red velvet cushions and decorative quilt. Dark wooden furnishings, dressing table, wardrobe and a solid chest of drawers all added to the flavour of a bygone age.

From the window we had an uninterrupted view of the magnificent gardens and grounds, the carefully tended rose bushes and magnolias in full bloom, the tall redwood trees and, in the distance, an ancient parish church that had served the local community and the Findlay family for many years.

We were novices, newcomers to the way of thinking here, but we could already sense something special about this magical place we had seemingly stumbled upon by chance. Little did we realise at the time what a profound impact Stansted, and all the amazing people we would encounter there over the years, would have on our lives.

Meanwhile, this extraordinary place exuded a unique and intriguing atmosphere. "If only the walls could speak..." we wondered. Here and there, engrained into the very fabric of the building, were reminders of an illustrious past: vintage framed sepia photographs and aged memorabilia told stories of amazing healers and mediums, many of whom may not have made the headlines but whose phenomenal gifts had become legend in the movement. The atmosphere was quite homely and hands-on, yet still richly imbued with characters, outstanding 'old school' mediums who graced the corridors and strutted the platform. Looking back, we realise just how blessed we were to encounter such exceptional talent and tap into their rare and special wisdom.

At six o'clock the dinner bell chimed. Mealtimes at Stansted were always a sense of occasion, we found, an opportunity to chat and get to know the other students on the course. The panelled dining room was cosy and intimate with tall, wide windows looking out onto the lawns and gardens, an ornate marble fireplace its centre piece, and a series of dark and rather serious-looking portraits on the walls that seemed to look down perhaps disapprovingly at the jovial banter and laughter that greeted us as we entered. It was all very quaint and old-fashioned. You could almost imagine the butler and maidservants scurrying back and forth from the kitchen and scullery, attending to the Findlay family and guests, serving fine food from silver platters. On this occasion, however, the service and atmosphere were rather less formal and protracted and more in keeping with the modern day.

We joined a table of eight and after brief good-humoured introductions quickly became involved in lively conversation with people from all backgrounds and walks of life. Everyone shared a common interest in spiritual growth and development and it was so refreshing to be able to converse freely without being concerned whether people understood what we were talking about. And what a motley crew we were. There was a young Welsh medium with a wicked sense of humour, a cheeky down-to-earth couple from Ealing who were very much into healing and an unusual young man from Birmingham sporting an amazing spikey, punk hairstyle – a professional jockey, he had swapped the equestrian lifestyle for a more spiritual calling. The whole atmosphere was warm and friendly. As soon as dinner was over, we all migrated to the library to discover our programme for the week.

Then all of a sudden the conversation stilled and a hush descended upon the room as the door opened and in walked Gordon Higginson, Principal of the College, President of the SNU and Course Organiser for the week. We had never seen or heard of Gordon but clearly he was held in awe by many of the students and we too were soon to be captured by his charm and charisma.

The programme for the week sounded fascinating: colour readings and aura assessments, one-to-ones and group work, lots of lectures and workshops and several demonstrations of mediumship. Having arrived here almost by accident, accepting an invitation for something we had never considered before, we suspected we were in for a treat… The sense of excitement among the group was palpable and, though some on the course were seasoned Spiritualists, many were newcomers like us, eager and hungry to learn. We retired to our bedroom pleasantly fatigued after a full and fascinating day, contemplating the treasures that lay ahead.

As the week unfolded we realised that the whole philosophy of this place was very much in keeping with what we had always thought, felt and believed. There was and still is a magic about Stansted Hall, a sense of the exceptional and the extraordinary and yet also a reassuring familiarity, a unique and special quality that even then, on our first visit, felt like we were 'coming home'.

The week just flew by. From dawn to dusk the packed programme engaged, inspired and stimulated us to want to know more. We were divided into small groups according to our experience, interests and, intriguingly, our 'psychic potential' and we met every afternoon in small rooms, attic spaces or, on sunny days, under the blossoming magnolia tree – always under the kind and watchful eye of our expert tutors. There was barely a minute to spare between the talks, demonstrations and group work and we loved very moment. It was all so new and yet strangely familiar, as though at a soul level we were meeting up with old friends and rediscovering what we already knew.

The spiritual menu on offer was too good to miss. We touched, tasted and tested all aspects of mediumship and psychic awareness from clairvoyance, clairaudience and clairsentience (seeing, hearing and sensing Spirit) to psychometry (sensing the energy of objects), aura readings, psychic art, spiritual healing, trance and physical mediumship. We sat in silence to build up the power, tuned into Spirit and meditated in the beautiful lounge, the sun streaming in through the large, ornate bay windows. It was in truth an idyllic week far removed from the noise and bustle of everyday life.

In between the talks, lectures and workshops we took time off to walk around the grounds and gardens, to bathe in the peace and energy, to appreciate the colours of the carefully tended flowerbeds, the scent of the roses and magnolias and to admire the tall American Redwood trees that towered majestically towards the sky. It was a time of reflection, discovery and revelation.

It was all very new and exciting for me, in fact quite a revelation. I had a little previous awareness of psychic phenomena and had made brief forays into spirituality, with a visit or two to the Findhorn Foundation in Scotland and taking an occasional yoga retreat in Devon or Dorset. I had always been fascinated by science fiction, the idea of time travel and the mysteries of the universe. When my father had become a healer, seemingly out of the blue, I had been initially sceptical, a curious bystander.[1] Subsequently I became intrigued and eventually totally drawn in and captivated by the extraordinary 'miracles' that were happening on my doorstep. But now, experiencing the many facets of spiritual and psychic gifts at first hand was an incredible eye-opening education, bringing Spirit 'alive' and opening up a whole new world of understanding for me.

"See what you can sense from this," suggested one of the tutors as she handed me a very old and worn Victorian-style ring. I had never done anything like this before and certainly do not claim any psychic ability, yet as soon as I held the ring in my hands I became aware of a strong and definite image in my mind's eye. At first I assumed it was my imagination at play.

"Just give what you get," encouraged my tutor. So I did. I had a strong impression, a vivid picture floating into my mind, of a beautiful turn of the last century schooner. I could 'see' the tall masts

---

[1]   See Previous Publications.

7

and billowing white sails, the immaculately polished wooden deck and, standing proudly on the deck attired in a smart blue blazer with braided cuffs, a stolid, upright-looking gentleman whom I assumed to be the captain. Sporting a thick white beard and tight curly hair, he looked every bit the part. What fascinated me was that the scene was not static. The captain was actually showing me around his boat and with great pride pointing out its various features. As my focus began to wane, my tutor encouraged me to continue.

"Does he have a message?" she suggested. I was still wondering whether I had perhaps imagined the whole thing, but when a lady in our group recognised the description as that of an old ancestor of hers, I took it far more seriously. I asked, mentally, if there was a message or purpose to my mystery guest's visit. The lady to whom the ring had belonged listened intently as I reeled off the thoughts that were coming into my mind without, as I was advised, trying to censor or evaluate them.

"He is telling me that you are about to go on a long trip and embark on a new venture. You have some doubts and trepidation but he is saying 'Don't worry, all will be well, it will be plain sailing.'" Imagine my surprise when she gratefully accepted everything I had said and explained that she had been asking for guidance and this answer had really helped her.

The energy at Stansted was so powerful that anything could happen, and more often than not it did. While we all – even me, apparently! – possess psychic faculties and potential to some extent that can be trained and developed with varying degrees of success, true spiritual mediumship is a gift to be equated with the artist, composer or musician. The unique artistry of being able to commune with Spirit, to bridge the dimensions of time and space and to bring the two worlds together, albeit temporarily, is a rare and special blessing not to be taken for granted.

Whilst the whole week was a revelation, there were one or two events that particularly stood out for us. On the Tuesday night, after sufficient tutoring and guidance, students were invited to share their fledgling psychic gifts with the whole class. When it came to Linda's turn, with Gordon Higginson standing protectively behind her and placing a reassuring hand on her shoulder, she could hardly believe the extraordinary flow of evidential information that gushed forth: words, images, thoughts and pictures of people and places she had never known or visited. It seemed as real as if she were watching an internal movie on the screen of her mind.

"Gordon stood behind me," Linda recalls, "and invited me to focus on someone in the room, to ask Spirit if there was a message for them. I was drawn to a young lady in the audience. I tuned in and asked for a message for her. I quickly became aware of a lady in the spirit world who had apparently been a cook in a kitchen. She was giving me the feeling that she knew this young lady when she was a schoolgirl and had come to recall their friendship and the fond memories they had shared." To Linda's surprise, the young woman completely understood the message and explained that she had attended a residential school and that the spirit lady had been the cook, someone who had taken great pride in her work and had become a special friend to her.

"It was an amazing feeling. I could see and feel the presence of Spirit as if they were right here in the room with us," she told me later.

They were just a subtle shift of consciousness away.
It is said the spirit dimension interweaves our own
but on a higher wavelength and vibration.
As we raise our vibration and they lower theirs,
so the two worlds may meet.

Sometimes the most evidential information may come when we least expect it and we may need to go away and check it out later. On the Wednesday evening, Gordon gave a public demonstration of mediumship in the Sanctuary and as always the room was packed with the ninety-plus students on our course and a healthy contingent of outside visitors.

"I've got someone here," he began, "with a strange foreign-sounding name." He slowly spelt out the letters one by one, pondering on each syllable: "P... O... D... E... M... S... K... Y." Then without hesitation he pointed towards Linda. "It's for you," he gesticulated, "but your name is Serlin, isn't it?"

Now, Podemsky is Linda's maiden name but we had booked into Stansted as the Serlins. Gordon continued, looking at Linda, who sat bolt upright in her chair listening carefully to his every word.

"I have your grandfather here." It was a very emotional moment. Linda had been very close to her grandfather and it was the first time she had ever received such a message since his passing. "He says he is with his parents and how happy they all are that you are here." Linda explained that this was our first visit to Stansted and that no-one else in her family really understood about Spirit or accepted these phenomena. Her grandfather had been a highly respected member of the community with strong and traditional religious beliefs so it was fascinating to learn that in the spirit world he had 'expanded his horizons' and become a wise counsel to all faiths. Gordon then referred to other members of the family in the spirit world, a Jacov and a Peral, whom Linda could not immediately identify; but a subsequent 'phone call to her Mum quickly confirmed their identity.

After Gordon's demonstration, Linda felt quite emotional. The thought that her grandparents were 'alive' was a profound and moving realisation. And we realised that it was not by chance that we had come to Stansted: there was a reason and a purpose behind our being drawn to this particular week, the full import of which would become apparent over time. Linda had actually been psychically aware from a very young age, though being at Stansted was now clearly amplifying and enhancing her innate ability.

"I would often have very vivid dreams," she later recalled. "I would be in the most beautiful places with vivid colours everywhere. I was aware of going into 'Halls of Learning' with many people sitting and listening to people speak. I just knew it was a visit to the spirit world, though I can't explain how I knew. At a very young age I knew that I was visiting somewhere I had been before I came to this physical world, a very familiar place.

"I had this sort of dream quite often and assumed at the time that everyone had the same type of experience. When I realised that other people did not have these experiences, I didn't talk about it because people might think I was odd. But it was a great help to me. If I was ever confused about anything, I would just put the question 'out there' and answers would come. I heard an inner voice. I would always get premonitions about things or find things that had been lost.

"One of the most vivid dreams I had was when my maternal grandfather Jack passed away. I was devastated. I was only fifteen at the time and my brother and I used to look after him because he had been involved in an accident and lost a leg and became somewhat incapacitated. My brother would help him bathe and I would shop and cook for him. We were very close to my grandfather and he lived very near us so I would see him often.

"When he passed away I was really very, very upset. A couple of days after he passed I sat on my bed crying. I was so upset and very sad. But that night I had the most amazing, vivid dream about my grandfather in which I saw him as a young man with two legs and hair – I had only known him as being bald. In this dream he said to me, 'Don't worry, darling. Now I can look after you! And I am very grateful to you for looking after me.'

"Interestingly, I told my mother about this dream and she accepted it and seemed to understand, although she was not necessarily psychically or spiritually aware. She was very comforted herself by this dream. Subsequent to that, my mother showed me a photograph of my grandfather as a young man and it was very much the picture of him I'd seen in my dream. Being psychically aware and tuned in to the spirit world is something I have always had, it seems. It has always been there and I'm very aware that I am intuitively guided. It has been an absolute treasure in my life."

Linda has always been passionate about colour (as evidenced by her wardrobe full of vibrant pinks and purples and stunning turquoise) so when she heard that effervescent Scottish medium Nita Saunders was presenting an afternoon workshop on The Power of Colour she booked herself a front row seat. Nita paced impatiently up and down the platform and talked with passion about her love of colour and how we can interpret colours to help and guide people along their life path. All of a sudden she stopped and looking at Linda, saying, "Why, young lady, I am being told that you could do what I am doing. Come up here on the platform."

Slightly bemused, Linda stepped up onto the platform, picked out a selection of brightly coloured ribbons and proceeded to give an impromptu yet inspired interpretation of their significance to a lady in the audience, who readily accepted all she was told. Nita was delighted with her new protégé, recognising the makings of an exceptional talent. That day in fact marked the beginning of an amazing gift for intuitive colour readings in Linda that was to blossom and grow over the years.

At the end of the incredible week we were treated to an aura reading and a one-to-one 'spiritual assessment' with Gordon, who insisted on giving a personal reading to everyone on the course. It was a daunting and time-consuming task, but one to which he was well accustomed. We waited patiently for our turn, which eventually came quite late in the evening. Gordon was tired and we felt guilty about taking up his time, but he relished the work and seemed indefatigable when it came to working with Spirit. To begin with he seemed far away as though looking at some distant object, then explained that he was scanning the different levels, layers and colours of our auras. We were fascinated, though a little apprehensive, as to what he might discover.

We were both told that we have powerful healing potential, that our energies are complementary and that we should work together.

Gordon told me, "For too long you have hidden your light under a bushel. Now is your time to shine and express your gifts. I see a book and lots of writing!" I was taken aback. My father was a well-known and respected healer but I had never really taken seriously the possibility that I too might be able to heal and I certainly had no plans at the time to write a book.

"You have a natural gift," he said, turning to Linda. "You can see and sense Spirit and have done since you were a child. You have many guides, helpers and inspirers from Spirit, a group of enlightened souls who draw near when you work with herbs and health. And I see you and David working in America… for Spirit but not necessarily within Spiritualism." We were rather bemused by what we were being told. We had never been to the States together and had no intention of doing so either; it all seemed fantastic and a little far-fetched, but we took away our package of predictions and agreed that time alone would tell.

It may have been the first but certainly was not the last time that we would visit Stansted Hall. Over the coming years, we would make many more visits both as students and even, eventually, as guest tutors. But this first out-of-the-blue encounter marked the turning point, the beginning of an amazing new chapter in our lives. Looking back, we can detect a golden thread, a divine plan unfolding that has brought into our lives a host of incredible teachers and mentors who have guided and inspired us along our spiritual path, among them people like Glyn Edwards, Judith Seaman and of course Gordon Higginson himself, who made such a profound and lasting impact on our lives.

By the way, what became of our new friends? Jean, from Ealing, became a popular Spiritualist platform medium whilst her husband Tom has dedicated his life to healing; and Eamon, the punk jockey, has since become a much in demand international medium of high repute. Linda herself has perfected her intuitive colour work and has been invited to present workshops to enthusiastic audiences in England, Geneva, Amsterdam and California.

Time and Space

*Every thought we think, every action we take, creates a ripple
on the surface of time. Nothing is 'by chance' where divine synchronicity
and the law of serendipity play their veiled and subtle part.
In Spirit – as we are given to understand – there is no time as we know it.
Time is a physical invention to contain and explain our physical world.
In Spirit there is just one continuous, infinite and eternal NOW
with everything happening 'at the same time'.*

*It is a confusing, even mind-boggling concept.
Imagine you are sitting in a railway carriage looking out of the window
and watching the countryside pass by. Your view of the world is framed by,
and limited to, what you can see through the window – this represents the
present. The countryside that has passed by and which you can no longer see
from your limited vantage point is the past. The countryside ahead of you,
which you cannot yet see, is the future.*

*Now imagine that instead of sitting in the carriage with a limited view and
perspective, you are sitting on top of the carriage with a much wider,
more panoramic view of the world. Everything around is happening
at the same time even though you may choose to focus your attention
on one aspect at a time. The past, present and future merge into one.
There is just the NOW.*

*This is how the mediumistic perspective perceives time and reality.
This is how, in the spirit world, the concept of time takes on
a whole new meaning. Whilst in the physical world our lives are controlled
by physical laws, scientific principles and age-old belief systems, these laws
and beliefs lose their meaning from a spiritual perspective.*

Love Never Dies

Gordon Higginson was a born medium. He lived, loved and breathed Spirit and was totally dedicated to the cause. When Linda and I first met him, we had felt an immediate connection, his warmth, humour and self-effacing charm quickly winning us over. There was something special about him, a certain quality, an air and presence – call it charisma. Whether it was his smile, twinkling blue eyes, neatly brushed back white hair or beautifully spoken, eloquent diction, he was well-loved and respected, even revered within the Spiritualist movement.

Apart from being Principal of the Arthur Findlay College, Gordon was also the longstanding President of the SNU. As if this were not enough, he was the President of his own church in Longton, near Stoke on Trent in Staffordshire, UK, where he lived and worked when he was not at Stansted Hall (which was much of the time) or on the road demonstrating his unique brand of mediumship to thousands of people all over the country (which was most of the time).

We quickly recognised that Gordon Higginson was a man of many qualities. A gifted medium, he also proved to be an incredibly inspiring and knowledgeable teacher with a rich heritage of wisdom and experience. We learned much from him in those early days. "Keep it simple," he would say. "Only accept what makes sense to you." And this was from a man adept at all forms of mediumship. He was a brilliant clairvoyant, giving remarkably detailed messages and descriptions in demonstrations that were always sold out. "I am really rather good, am I not?" he would quip with an ironic self-deprecating smile. But, yes, Gordon was possibly one of the foremost mediums in the world at the time. He was not tempted by fame or fortune or international repute, but was content to serve Spirit in whatever way he could.

He was also an incredible trance medium, a form of mediumship whereby the medium becomes overshadowed by a spirit being or, in a deeper trance state, allows a spirit to communicate through him or her. Once we had become accustomed to the idea, we enjoyed listening to the whimsical wisdom of Gordon's Chinese guide or the cheeky banter from an Irishman called Paddy.

Most impressively, Gordon was also an outstanding physical medium, a form of mediumship rarely seen these days but which in its heyday produced some phenomenal results such as 'direct voice' (described just before the first chapter) and even the materialisation of spirit beings. Gordon was a spiritual workaholic too, often staying up well into the night giving one-to-one readings and aura assessments to his students, such as the memorable session for Linda and me.

We feel blessed and privileged to have known Gordon and to count him as a special friend and spiritual mentor. He had a soft spot for Linda and would often stand behind her stroking her long dark hair, which apparently reminded him of his mother, Fanny, to whom he was devoted. He would often tease Linda about her enthusiasm for nutrition and healthy eating. Like many modern mediums he was on the road a lot, rarely at home, and often at the mercy of well-meaning but not always the healthiest hospitality.

"I love vegetarian food," he would begin seriously. "I will eat a healthy vegetarian meal… and then have my meat and two veg!" On one occasion, after Linda had presented a Healthy Lifestyle workshop, Gordon shared a little confession: "I was walking through the town when I came across a cake shop. The smell of the fresh baking was so tempting and the sight of those cream cakes and buns… well, I could hardly contain myself when psychically I heard a voice…" Everyone wondered what he was going to say. "It was Linda Serlin and she was saying 'NO, Gordon!'" Everyone laughed. He had a great sense of humour and, while he did not take himself too seriously, he had a great deal of respect for Linda's passion and commitment. "She is so enthusiastic!" He was the first to admit that he needed nutritional help but did not have the intention, or willpower, to follow it through.

Gordon shared an amusing tale about the time he was asked to take the funeral service for a well-to-do old lady whom he had known for many years. The congregation gathered, family and friends, at the local Spiritualist church while the coffin containing the mortal remains of the old lady was wheeled in. Gordon was standing on the platform preparing his talk when he noticed, psychically, the spirit of the old lady herself sitting in the front row with a distinctly disgruntled look on her face! It was obviously quite disconcerting and distracting for Gordon, but he endeavoured to continue with his carefully rehearsed few lines. The old lady in spirit, however, was determined to interrupt proceedings and grab Gordon's attention.

"See this lot here," she said to him, pointing at the assembled crowd and swearing in no uncertain terms. "They didn't want to know me when I was alive and now I'm dead they've all turned up to see what they can scrounge off me!"

Gordon couldn't help but see the funny side of it and did what he could to placate the lady while continuing resolutely with his sermon, trying in vain to keep a straight face. The moral of the story is, of course, that while she might have been so-called dead the old lady was apparently alive, alert and aware in the spirit world and knew exactly what was going on. To the uninitiated this story might seem bizarre, even beyond belief, but to a seasoned medium like Gordon an experience like this was almost commonplace.

'Keep it simple' became our spiritual mantra. Many people, it seems, get caught up in complicated jargon and weird and wonderful ideas that just do not make sense. There is a law and a principle in Spirit, Gordon would explain, that is perfectly logical and natural:

We are, in essence, Spirit here and now
clothed in a physical body for this experience of life.

When people pass on they retain all their characteristics, memories and personality traits, then gradually they progress and evolve into an expanded vision of life. "But don't expect them all suddenly to become saints and sages!"

Gordon reminded us that communication between the different dimensions, though perfectly natural, is not easy. Spirit people must learn how to 'lower their vibration' and have to learn a whole new language in order to communicate, through a medium, to loved ones here on Earth. We have to be patient, and recognise moreover that when people move on to the spiritual plane they lead busy, full and active lives and do not always have either the 'time' or inclination to return to this slower, denser vibration to give us a message.

The lessons we learned through Gordon's talks, demonstrations and one-to-one sessions were fundamental to our awareness and understanding of the nature of Spirit. We feel blessed to have had the opportunity to spend time with such a wise and inspiring teacher. We know that our own spiritual journey began in earnest the day we first discovered Stansted Hall and met Gordon Higginson.

It was a chilly November evening with a brisk wind blowing as we gathered in the lobby at Stansted for a physical mediumship séance with Gordon. A flickering fire sent shadows across the crowded room and set the scene for the bizarre event we were about to experience. Demonstrations of physical mediumship, in which the medium endeavours to provide objective evidence of survival, were few and far between and we felt privileged to have been invited there that night. We had heard stories of the extraordinary manifestations purported to have taken place at some of Gordon's previous séances, but we came with an open mind. Little did we realise that this would be one of Gordon's final séances as this form of mediumship is very demanding and had already taken its toll on his health.

At 7.30 p.m. the door to the library was opened and we filed in slowly and quietly, respecting the silence of this hallowed space. There were several rows of seats carefully laid out in a crescent shape and, in one corner, a small curtained cabinet in which Gordon sat. He was dressed in black, presumably so that we may more easily discern the white ectoplasm, should it occur. By his side sat two trusted mediums holding his hands. The atmosphere was tense and exciting. We had never experienced anything quite like this before.

The door was closed and secured so that the proceedings would not be disturbed. We were asked not to talk or make any sudden noises that may harm the medium. The lights were dimmed so that there was just the faint, warm, red glow from a lamp in the corner. Music began, songs were sung with rousing tunes 'to raise the energy', and then there was silence. Gordon appeared to have fallen into a deep, trance-like sleep. We sat quietly attentive, holding our breath, wondering what was going to happen next.

Seconds passed that seemed like minutes and then from one corner of the room, or so it seemed, came a disembodied, high-pitched and sing-song voice. In any other context one might have been sceptical but this was objective evidence of Spirit, the voice belonging to Gordon's spirit guide endearingly called Cuckoo. Although she came across as quite childlike, this was only a persona, the means by which she chose to present herself as she was without doubt – we came to realise – a very wise and mature soul. (It was later explained that a 'psychic voice box' has to be created using spirit substances and Gordon's energies to facilitate such voice communication.)

It seemed quite incredible. We sat there listening to Gordon's guide giving a running commentary on proceedings, while Gordon apparently slept. Cuckoo explained that it was her job to organise things in the spirit world, to ensure that Gordon was safe and well looked after, that conditions were as good as possible and that the string of spirit people urging and nudging her in the background might get a chance to communicate. She also explained that this kind of mediumship was not easy, that we should be patient, that every séance was an experiment and that results could not be guaranteed. Then, with an endearing little chuckle that evoked smiles all round, she retreated into the background and silence fell again.

Suddenly the mood changed. There was a discernible shift in the energy, a deepening and a cooling of the atmosphere feeling like an icy cold draught around our legs. We nudged one another, holding back any words, fully focused on what was happening. And what followed was a moving and memorable experience that we shall never forget.

As if from far away, a different voice echoed from an empty corner of the room, faint at first like a whisper, straining for breath and almost choking with emotion. Gradually it gained strength.

"Lily… are you there?" the voice pleaded. "It's… John… It's me… I am here."

An elderly white-haired lady in the front row cried out in joy, recognising the voice of her late husband.

"John! Is that really you?" Her tears of relief and love flowed. There followed a slight pause as if the spirit communicator were mustering his energy for another try. There were no profound words of wisdom or dramatic insights, just three simple, poignant words.

"I love... you..."

Then the energy of John's voice seemed to falter and fade as if the emotional intensity of the situation had overwhelmed him and the connection was lost. There was silence in the room save for the tears of joy of the lady who had heard her husband's voice again after so many years.

Everyone in the room was stunned and moved to have been privy to this extraordinary and intimate reunion.

Had that been it, it would have been enough. But there was more.

The room became quiet again except for a peculiar rustling sound. We couldn't tell what it was or where it was coming from, but as it got louder there was a palpable shift in the energy, a step up in gear. A blanket of warmth enveloped the room and we sensed something special was about to happen. As we craned our necks to see through the faint red glow of the lamp, we noticed something amazing taking place around Gordon. For a moment or two we could not see his face, which seemed to be shrouded in a white haze, and then all around him and seemingly emanating from him were billowing clouds of white, gossamer-like, ectoplasmic material. It is difficult to describe, perhaps like muslin or with the texture of candy floss, dancing, flowing, floating, hovering inches above the floor.

"So this," I was thinking, "must be the stuff that ghosts are made of."

The dancing cloud of spirit substance seemed to deepen in intensity and build up until it was over five feet high. Cuckoo intervened here and explained that, hopefully, the patiently waiting spirit people would be able to impress themselves – their face, form and personality – into this substance like a sort of spiritual mould. We could hear her encouraging, urging and occasionally cajoling the waiting spirits to work harder, to push more firmly and to use the energy better. Just a few days earlier, we could not have imagined witnessing such a supernatural performance being played out before our very eyes.

But then the white cloud began to fade, melting slowly away as the energy gradually dissipated and dissolved like melting ice. We could sense Cuckoo's frustration and disappointment, but she calmly explained that it was taking too much out of the medium and she could not risk harming him, his wellbeing her prime concern. Nevertheless, we had still experienced the most incredible demonstration of psychic power, the manifestation of ectoplasm and direct voice communication. We were both a little dazed and overwhelmed, trying to take in the implications of what we had just seen and would never forget.

Gordon slowly returned to normal consciousness, drank a glass of water and, with a deep yawn and shudder, was slowly helped to his feet by his two trusted aides. Before leaving the room, he turned to the audience.

"I do hope you enjoyed this evening and your experience of Spirit."

The ninety or so people in the room filed out slowly and silently, in awe of the remarkable phenomena we had experienced. Even so, it wasn't quite over yet... Bright and early the following morning, some beautiful tiny, exotic flowers appeared on the floor of the library, apparently psychic 'apports', transmuted by Spirit through time and space as gifts from another dimension and reminders that love never dies.

We were learning that we are Spirit here and now,
spiritual beings having a human experience.
We are pure energy, and energy never dies, it just changes form.
We existed before this lifetime and will continue to exist,
moving inexorably from one level of consciousness to another.

New Dimensions

We had just returned from a week in the Canaries, our favourite off-season retreat, to find an unusual message on our answerphone. We were taken aback to hear the unmistakeable voice of Gordon Higginson inviting us to be guest tutors on one of his special Healing Weeks at Stansted. We played the tape over again just to make sure. Yes, it was definitely Gordon's voice and, yes, we had definitely been invited to join his course. To receive a personal invitation from him, the top man at Stansted and of the SNU, was no mean thing and to be honest it was quite overwhelming. The following day, a letter arrived from his secretary formally confirming the details. We were absolutely thrilled at the prospect and wasted no time in responding with an enthusiastic "Yes!"

It had by now been a few years since our first life-changing visit to Stansted and there had been a lot of water under the bridge. Linda and I had embarked on our own healing journey and after a rigorous two-year probationary course with dozens of patients' testimonials and the helpful guidance of our sponsor, Ray, we had qualified as spiritual healers with the National Federation of Spiritual Healers, an organisation founded by the late and great Harry Edwards.

Linda had also pursued and developed her interests in nutrition and colour, whilst I had studied and qualified as a Positive Thinking teacher with the Peiffer Foundation[2]. Clearly, Gordon had indeed seen some serious potential in our auras. In all honesty, we now felt qualified, experienced and ready for the challenge.

Apart from being a remarkable medium, Gordon was passionate about promoting all aspects of healing and had a grand vision of creating a Holistic Healing Centre in the grounds of Stansted, bringing together the various strands of alternative, complementary and spiritual healing under one roof. His special Healing Weeks were intended as stepping stones to this greater goal (although, sadly, it was not to be realised in his lifetime). Gordon was breaking new ground by inviting non-SNU healers and practitioners to be on his course, but then he enjoyed ruffling a few feathers and was keen to experiment and to innovate.

These courses turned out to be a lot of work and a lot of fun. Gordon seemed to have inexhaustible energy when it came to working with Spirit and was always keen to explore new ideas and approaches, his energy and enthusiasm infectious. He was a total source of inspiration and an absolute pleasure to work with. We felt blessed to be able to spend time in his presence and learn from his wisdom and experience.

We were busy from dawn to dusk giving talks, leading workshops and groups, and doing one-to-one sessions; it was a packed schedule punctuated by fleeting meetings in the staffroom to discuss progress and the inevitable last-minute alterations and impromptu additions to the programme.

---

[2] The Peiffer Foundation was set up in 1994 by Vera Peiffer, a psychotherapist and author of many books, with the aim of promoting personal development.

"Give it a try," Gordon would suggest, keen to encourage and push the barriers, "You can do it." We were left very much to our own devices but Gordon knew intuitively who could best do what, and it worked.

On offer was an exciting and enlightening mix of therapies and healing modalities from acupuncture and aromatherapy to the Bowen Technique, massage and meditation, drumming and dowsing, hypnotherapy, shamanic dance, colour therapy, nutrition and spiritual healing.

Linda gathered a healthy following for her workshops and personal sessions, among them Glyn Edwards, a protégé of Gordon's and an outstanding medium in his own right. Glyn was a very colourful and flamboyant character whose hectic lifestyle became duly subsidised by regular infusions of delicious Bio-Strath Health Tonics, generously supplied by Linda from her rapidly dwindling treasure chest of healthy goodies. Linda was keen to encourage the mediums to supplement with healthy tonics instead of the more traditional cups of tea or coffee laden with sugar. Glyn became an avid disciple and a good friend, and conjured up some intriguing experiments to assess the relative life force energy of organic and non-organic foods; and guess what, the organic won hands down. Glyn subsequently invited us to present a Healthy Living seminar at his church in the heart of Liverpool. It was a glorious weekend and Linda rose to the occasion as she bravely endeavoured to talk about tofu, nut rissoles and vegetarian schnitzels to a hall packed full of no-nonsense northerners! As it happens, humour prevailed and Linda's talks went down a treat, her sheer energy and enthusiasm making many new converts.

Stansted was all about 'energy' and on a Wednesday we had the opportunity to explore energy of a different kind, the afternoon being designated free time and an opportunity for students to stretch their wings and see the town. But no-one wanted to leave or break the spell because we were all having such a good time. Nothing was scheduled on the programme so, in a moment of inspiration, Gordon suggested, "The library is available so why don't you two arrange something special for this afternoon?" We had nothing prepared but an idea came to mind that we had been toying with for a while. With Gordon's blessing and Spirit's backing we accepted the invitation.

The word spread quickly. There would be a Healing Meditation with David and Linda Serlin in the library at three o'clock. We had expected twenty to thirty people but over sixty students turned up. Chairs were arranged in a circle, some gentle, relaxing music was played (Mike Rowland's *Silver Wings* fitted the bill perfectly), we lit a candle and proceeded to guide our crew into a deep relaxation followed by a meditative journey into the angelic realms. Curtains drawn and lights dimmed with just the flickering incandescent glow from a solitary candle, the scene was set for an extraordinary healing journey.

Before long we were all floating on imaginary clouds, disappearing into a heavenly cosmos. The atmosphere was perfect for a healing fountain, embracing everyone in a powerful healing energy and sending out streams of light into the world. Our group of sixty became as one. No-one wanted to move or speak, such was the gorgeous, serene energy that circulated round the room, connecting each one to another. Holding on to the power, we placed two chairs in the centre of the circle for anyone who wanted or needed hands-on healing. There was no shortage of takers and Linda and I literally had our hands full moving gently from one person to another, feeling the connection, channelling the energy, letting Spirit do the work. And there was no shortage of Spirit that afternoon. The library was buzzing with energy and so were we. We lost all track of time as the hour and half session flew by. A latecomer noted the incredible atmosphere in the room.

"What's been going on here?" she enquired, wondering what she had missed. As we turned on the lights and opened the curtains to let in the early evening light, we recognised that something special had taken place.

"That was wonderful," commented one of the students. "I feel great, and my back pain has completely disappeared!"

"I hear your Healing Meditation was a great success," remarked Gordon the next day. "You must do it again." And we did. But this time in a completely different environment and context.

We felt inspired to try a repeat performance at our home, now in Stanmore, Middlesex, and earmarked a Sunday evening for our inaugural event, inviting interested friends to bring their family and friends. On the night we had a full house with over twenty-five people. We used the same format that had proved so popular and effective at Stansted, and with a smaller group the results were even more intense. Bearing in mind that many of our guests were new to spiritual ideas, the relaxation, guided meditation and distant healing fountain went down a treat; and everyone had the opportunity to receive hands-on healing from Linda and me and to feel part of proceedings.

Linda and I had recently moved from our compact basement flat on the outskirts of Hampstead, where Keats and Freud had once lived, to this more sedate north-west London suburb, best known perhaps as the setting for Bentley Priory, the home and base for wartime leader Lord Dowding (himself a Spiritualist) and from where he had devised the successful outcome to the Battle of Britain.

We had also married and embarked with unbridled enthusiasm on our spiritual journey together. I must confess, looking back, that it has been an absolute blessing, and still is, to share the journey with someone so special. We are best friends too and I can recall the magical evening when a voice from Spirit – I am convinced it was my grandmother – urged me, "Don't let this one go." I didn't and the rest, as they say, is history.

As we prepared for our Sunday evening Healing Meditations we were very much aware of the presence of Spirit. These evenings proved very popular and soon became a regular feature in many diaries. News spread fast and before long an increasing number of people were getting in touch, some with significant health problems, hoping to experience spiritual healing for themselves. The feedback was gratifying and the results were encouraging, in some cases quite outstanding.

"I would like to say how much Linda and David have helped me over an extremely painful period in my life." SL

"I am writing to say a huge 'Thank You'. I had been most unwell. My nerves were on edge and I had severe problems with my ears. Noises from outside became magnified to such an extent that I would have to go to bed and hide away. During the first healing evening that I came to I remember sitting in a chair and became aware of a tremendous heat coming from your hands which were near my ears. The heat felt soothing and subsequently after attending a few more evenings I am completely recovered! 'Thank you' really is an inadequate word for the way I would like to express my thanks to you." LC

"I and my family have received great comfort as a result of Linda and David's healing treatment for different ailments. My daughter had severely burned her hands with boiling oil. She had deep and painful burns which were healing very slowly and giving her a great deal of pain. After receiving healing from Linda and David they healed with dramatic quickness! In fact, by the next morning there was no more stiffness or pain. Her hands had healed completely leaving no scars even though the doctors had warned that they would probably be scarred. Everyone who has received healing from Linda and David have benefitted greatly." MC

"I received healing from David and Linda for a longstanding lower back problem. I sat on a chair and David and Linda positioned

themselves behind me. I closed my eyes to avoid distractions. I did not know what to expect. Straight away I felt a tremendous sensation of warmth around the top of my head. I felt heat travel slowly down my back passing through my spine to the lower back area. The overall sensation was as if a warm, comforting hot water bottle had been activated within my body. I could feel strains, aches and pains, both mental and physical, draining away. After the healing the pain had gone completely. As a result, my backache, which had been quite painful, was greatly relieved and several weeks after receiving healing is still much better. I would repeat the experience. Thank you." DB

Linda and I practise spiritual healing. We do not make any promises or predict any specific result. We just pray for the best possible outcome and leave the rest to Spirit. Healing takes many different forms and may provide a catalyst for positive change in all kinds of situations. It works when we let go and put the matter in the hands of Spirit. For example, a neighbour struck a forlorn figure standing in the doorway, clearly in pain and hardly able to walk. Somehow, she had managed to shuffle the hundred yards or so from her home to ask for healing. Apparently, she had been stretching up to close a curtain when she had suffered a sudden spasm of pain in her back, so bad that she had screamed and fallen to the floor.

"Never in my life had I felt such pain," she said later. "I was unable to walk apart from moving slowly to the kitchen or bathroom. I was desperate so I went to see a chiropractor, but the pain persisted and a few days later became even worse in my back and hip and running down my leg. I felt depressed and exhausted, particularly as it was my birthday. But somehow I managed to walk to David and Linda's house to ask for healing.

"As soon as I saw David and Linda, the pain in my back and hip began to ease. At the healing session that followed I felt a lot of heat in my lower back, which already felt lighter and calmer and after two more sessions all the pains had gone. Apart from feeling tired I was better. I realised that my body had rebelled against years of stress and struggle. The positive side of my illness, however, was that it made me slow down and reassess my life." RC

Linda and I enjoy working together as a team, our energies seem to be compatible and complementary, and we will often finish an evening feeling more energised and refreshed than when we had started! We realise that, essentially, we are channels through whom spirit guides and doctors may do their work, focusing the healing energy that emanates, we believe, from an altogether higher Source.

It was immensely gratifying to receive the positive feedback and to hear that, sometimes, people sitting quietly in the background and not apparently receiving healing would report amazing improvements in health conditions they hadn't even have mentioned. Such is the Power for Good.

The apparent simplicity of healing, however, disguises a deeper and more profound potential, limited only by what we believe to be possible. Sometimes the most profound healings take place quite spontaneously with little fuss or preparation, when we just let go and let God act.

We have come to believe that healing emanates from an altogether higher Source and we are but the channels, the focal points for divine spiritual energy. Yet it is our uniqueness that lends each healing a personal quality, a special flavour all of its own.

We were beginning to learn about other dimensions of life, other levels of consciousness. The following bizarre manifestation is an example.

"Take a look at these," my father suggested, presenting me with a set of colourful family photographs. "Notice anything unusual about them?" I was curious, sure that this must be a trick question, so I scrutinised the prints searching for some obvious anomaly but could find nothing suspicious. "Have another look," he urged with a wry grin on his face. Then I saw it – how could I have missed it?

The photos comprised a set of four prints, each taken one after another on a sunny afternoon at my parents' home. The time was clearly marked on the back of each print and ranged from 4.13 p.m. to 4.15 p.m. There were four people in the picture, my mother and my three nieces. My father had taken the pictures.

There it was, sticking out like a sore thumb at a top corner of the first photograph was a clearly visible, peculiar white object. It looked at first glance like a bundle of fluff. On the second picture, taken several seconds later, the mysterious object had apparently moved; it was now higher up in the picture and seemed to have sprouted legs and a head! Moreover, around it were several green fronds like the leaves of a rubber plant – but there were no plants in the kitchen. The object looked solid and even seemed to cast a shadow over a toaster on the nearby breakfast bar. On the third photo, taken one minute after the first, the mysterious object had dropped lower and seemed to be staring at my mother and my nieces. Then in the fourth image it had completely disappeared.

I was intrigued. What on Earth was this mystery object and where had it come from? It could not have been something thrown across the room, as that would have taken a second or two, would obviously have been noticed and would have fallen to the floor. What puzzled me most were the green fronds emanating from it.

When I turned the picture upside down, however, I got a surprise. The mystery object looked uncannily like a fluffy, white lamb, or...

Then I got it. The head, the legs, the semblance of a collar around the neck and the fluffy white fur: it was a miniature white poodle. One could even just see the head and mouth. Many years before, my mother had had a pretty white poodle called Pepe, of which she was incredibly fond. Indeed, Pepe had become like one of the family. Could this bizarre manifestation, for which we could find no logical explanation, really be the fleeting spirit return of this dog?

Before rushing to any conclusions, however, we sought to rule out all other possibilities such as a mark or blemish on the print or some dust on the camera lens, so we sent the prints to an expert laboratory for close scrutiny. They confirmed that the prints were in perfect order and that there were no signs of distortion; if there had been, they would be uniform on all the prints. The official conclusion sent a shiver down our spine and confirmed our suspicions.

"It must be a ghost," they said.

Still not being wholly satisfied, we sent the prints to a team of well known and respected psychics who confirmed that, in their opinion, this was one of the most vivid and solid examples in print of a spirit manifestation. The green fronds, apparently, were bands of psychic energy.

We were baffled by these extraordinary photographs. In the absence of any other credible explanation, we all had to conclude that this was indeed a psychic phenomenon and that our dog Pepe had made a brief but noticeable return to the family he loved. Somehow, the convergence of a unique set of psychic energies had enabled this to happen, opening a temporary 'portal' into the world beyond. It showed us that even animals live on in Spirit and that love can bridge the dimensions.

Linda looked perplexed. She had recently seen a medium and brought home a tape recording of the session, but the message made no sense.

It was something about a grey-haired lady who had lived in a flat near a hill in the countryside. The whole thing seemed like a waste of time and she was just about to discard the recording she had been given when I stopped her.

"Hold on a moment, that sounds like my grandmother, Marie. Let's listen to the tape together."

Far from being useless, the message turned out to be extremely evidential and quite fascinating. And the fact that Linda had never known my grandmother reinforced the integrity of the information. Marie had lived in a flat in Hertfordshire, a stone's throw from what was called Garrison Hill. She was a sweet and caring person but, as far as I could recall, always seemed to be ill and the regular visits to the doctor had become the highlight of her week. Notwithstanding, she rarely complained, was loved by everyone who knew her and just got on with life as best she could. Looking back, I suspect she must have felt incredibly frustrated and unfulfilled.

Apparently, she was using this opportunity to welcome Linda into the family and to talk about her new life since she had passed to the spirit world. Marie explained through the medium that, now she was freed from the burden of her many physical ailments, she was able to pursue and fulfil many of her lifetime's dreams and ambitions, including running a nursery for spirit children. Whilst it seemed almost too good to be true, Marie seemed happy and contented now and was leading a very full, busy and active life in Spirit.

Also in the taped message was an equally interesting and heart-warming story about my late grandfather, Joseph. A skilled tailor by profession, Joseph had ended up working in a local factory and I recall seeing him riding to work on his rusty bicycle and returning home at night, weary and jaded with a rough stubble on his chin.

No-one ever knew about – and he never gave the slightest intimation of – his real interest and passion, which was to play the piano. We now discovered that in his new life Joseph was using his 'time' to study and play the piano under the guidance and tutelage of some of the grand masters.

As a child, I had spent many happy holidays in Hitchin with my grandparents, but it had never occurred to me how limited and restricted their lives must have been. It was a profound revelation, therefore, to learn just how expanded and fulfilled their lives had become in the spirit world.

Life moves inexorably from one level of consciousness to another. The ability to communicate through the dimensions, to reconnect with friends and loved ones who have passed on, to receive counsel, inspiration and support from higher minds, is a gift to be cherished. As we lift the veil, the two worlds may meet for we are all connected.

In our spiritual endeavours, our contemplation, prayer and practice, we seek to align with the infinite, our divine Source. If we listen carefully, in the silence we may discern that still small voice within that seeks to show us the way, even where there seemed to be no way. In an ever-changing world, the one constant, never-changing truth is Spirit.

Today, we are at a crossroads. We can choose to acknowledge our spiritual heritage, purpose and potential, or remain embedded in tribal consciousness and limiting beliefs. It only takes one candle to light a room, one enlightened soul to change the focus and lift the energy to an altogether higher level. Within each of us lies limitless power and potential so it is up to us to recognise it, become aware of it and choose how we may use it for the highest good of all.

Gordon Higginson with Linda at Stansted Hall

Stansted Hall, Essex, UK

There are many interesting and varied interpretations of the nature of life in the spirit world. Heaven, it is said, is not a place but a state of consciousness. My own research and experience has led me to the understanding that the spirit world functions on a different dimension or wavelength to that of the Earth, a higher vibration beyond the comprehension of our five physical senses. It takes the special senses of a psychic or a spiritual medium to pierce the veil and peer into the higher realms of being, although many people claim to have experienced spontaneous, fleeting glimpses of Spirit, moments when the dimensions seem to overlap and the two worlds temporarily meet.

We are pure energy and energy never dies, it just changes form. Think of it like this. Imagine a simple desktop fan sitting silent and still; even when you turn it on at its lowest setting the blades move slowly and appear solid and visible to the naked eye. Then as you turn up the setting, the blades oscillate faster, their vibration rises and they appear invisible. Spirit functions at a higher vibration. In order to communicate with us, usually through a medium, and make their presence known, those in the spirit world must temporarily lower their vibration to match the denser, heavier vibration of Earth.

To really understand the nature of Spirit we have to shift our perception and use our imagination. Everything we see and know as solid matter is, in reality, a swirling mass of energy and atomic particles, lumped together to form familiar, identifiable objects. Spirit people may see us, then, as emanations of light and energy whilst, to each other, they apparently have identifiable form (albeit non-physical), character and personality. I am reminded of a wonderful film called *Cocoon* in which a team of aliens arrive on Earth cloaked in temporary human bodies, which they discard as soon as they are alone to reveal their original, pure and stunning energy bodies with which they can express their true selves, free and unencumbered.

In the spirit world, the power of thought is paramount. With no limitations of time or space, thoughts become things instantly. Ideas, intentions and desires manifest and materialise. It is said that people gravitate to the level of their own consciousness and literally create their own environment by their thoughts and beliefs. Like attracts like. There is still free will, of course, so we may choose to grow and develop through endless opportunities and invitations.

Without any physical encumbrances, people shed all physical ailments and debilities and return to their prime; this explains why sometimes we may dream of people who have passed on but see them as much younger and more vibrant editions of themselves.

We are told by spirit communicators of amazing edifices and structures, beautiful temples and Halls of Learning, stunning landscapes and gardens with the most exquisite flowers, shrubs and colours so breathtakingly beautiful that there are no words to describe them. It is as if the beauty we see on Earth is but a reflection, a mere shadow, of an original heavenly blueprint.

As above, so below. As in Heaven, so too on Earth. The power of thought is paramount here too. We are constantly creating our own experience through our thoughts, beliefs and attitudes. We too are blessed with free will and the power of choice to accept or refuse the invitations and opportunities that come our way. We are here to learn life's lessons, after all, to grow and evolve spiritually, to enjoy a material life, to find joy in simple things and to experience love in its many forms and guises.

Having grasped new opportunities, Linda and I felt it important to have a place of pilgrimage, somewhere to go to be spiritually recharged and renewed. Stansted had become such a place for us as right from the start it had felt like we were coming home.

After years of use as a centre for spiritual study, the essence of Spirit has become imbued into the very fabric of the building. Echoes of the past linger around every corner, inscribed on the back of a bench or on a wooden dedication plaque tucked discretely amongst the rose bushes. Portraits of past masters hang on the walls in the lounge and lobby and

I have always particularly liked the one of Gordon Higginson smiling, watching over us from the wall in the library. We continued to visit regularly. The names and faces may change but the feeling remained, reminders of the many wonderful times we have spent there: the many courses, the amazing people met over the years, the extraordinary experiences and above all the fun and the laughter.

At the end of a busy full-on week there would often be a party, concert or celebration, a time to let our hair down. The mark of a great spiritual teacher, it seems to me, is their sense of humour and ability not to take themselves too seriously. Gordon enjoyed a good laugh and was always willing to join in the celebrations, whether it was a hearty sing-song or an energetic dance routine. There was a hilarious incident once when we were doing a sacred circle dance, with steps that were intricate and challenging. Gordon insisted on joining in although he was not quite as graceful as a swan. Holding hands with Linda, he seemed to have missed his step, lost his rhythm and started bobbing up and down out of time like a yo-yo. Seeing the funny side, however, Gordon made a joke of it and gleefully exclaimed, "Bob-Bob-Bob-Bob." Even the sacred can be fun.

On another occasion we played a psychic version of the popular TV show *Blind Date*. Gordon was seated in a chair with a row of raucous ladies seeking to attract his attention and secure a date. The resulting mêlée was hilarious with the audience in uproar. Gordon was flushed with embarrassment, 'though I'm sure he secretly enjoyed all the attention.

Over the years we met some exceptional people at Stansted and made many lasting friendships, amongst them a very special couple from Newcastle we fondly called 'our Northern Lights'. Carol and Colin shared our cheeky sense of humour and, when it came to the end-of-week concert, they were eager to get together with us to perform. In a moment of inspiration, we called our newly formed group The Crystal Balls. What we might have lacked in singing prowess we made up for in enthusiasm, with a mission to entertain at all costs. Our motto: "No venue too small, no fee too large."

We rehearsed dutifully and in between the chuckles and belly laughs created an impressive programme of music and songs, putting a subtle psychic twist on some old favourites. We wanted to do something different and, with two budding psychics Linda and Carol in our midst, it was hardly surprising that the end result was not quite what one would have expected. Concert night arrived and we all gathered in the lobby at Stansted looking forward to an entertaining evening of music, dance and humour. The first few acts were great fun and helped set the mood with some outstanding virtuoso performances and cameo appearances by some of the mediums.

Then it was time for The Crystal Balls. We kicked off with an updated version of an old Drifters' hit, *Save the Last Trance for Me*. The audience quickly cottoned on to what we were doing and warmly received our next number, dedicated to our medium friend Judith Seaman, the classic Beatles' tune, *Hey Jude*. What happened next, however, was quite uncanny. We had geared our song choices specifically for each of the mediums. When it came to a song for Joan, a lovely lady from Wales, for some reason *Hello Dolly* had come to mind. As we got into the swing of it, we noticed that Joan was looking a bit unsettled.

"How did you know?" she gasped. It seems that this song had a particular and very special significance for her. As a naturally psychic child she had often engaged in imaginary conversations with her little doll and always began the dialogue with the words "Hello dolly". When we followed up with an a cappella version of *Puff The Magic Dragon* she nearly fell off her chair, because that was one of her favourite childhood songs too.

Who said spirituality has to be serious? We met many colourful and charismatic characters at Stansted and you could almost make a film of it. Funnily enough…

One day, we had just arrived at Stansted laden with luggage ready for a peaceful and relaxing week, or so we thought, to be met by a barrage of blazing lights and booming voices.

39

"Can you go out and come back in again?" a strange voice bellowed.

What on Earth was going on? We wondered whether we had walked into the wrong course. It certainly wasn't the sort of welcome we were accustomed to. Then someone explained to us that the BBC were filming for a forthcoming TV documentary. A film crew had established themselves with all their paraphernalia in the reception lobby and we had landed right in the middle of things. They wanted to show a typical week at the college from when one arrived to the end. To begin within it was all quite unsettling, but we soon got used to the idea and after signing the usual disclaimer forms (did we mind being filmed?) we actually got caught up in the excitement of the organised chaos. Naturally, Linda wondered whether she had brought enough changes of outfits; after all, we could be featured in a full-length TV spectacular!

There were cameras and boom mikes everywhere, film crews around every corner and present at every talk, workshop and demon-stration. After the initial surprise, we got used to seeing them hanging around and asking all sorts of questions. They were actually quite a nice crowd and one of the young female producers became actively and enthusiastically involved in the course herself, particularly after being told she had mediumistic potential.

Linda and I were interviewed about how we had discovered Spiritualism. It was intriguing to sit on the other side of a camera and, at first, I did feel rather self-conscious but then actually enjoyed the process. We learned from the producers that the film was due for screening later that year as part of a documentary series, but the final cut, the theme and emphasis would be down to the director, who would select the material that best supported whatever angle he or she had in mind.

It was a lively and fun week and despite the distractions of the omnipresent cameras and microphones it turned out to be a very con-genial and good-humoured one. We were really excited about seeing the finished product, 'though at the back of our minds was a lingering doubt as to how the film might portray the course, the college, the students and Spiritualism in general. The film crew had thoroughly enjoyed themselves and parted with waves and smiles all round. Several months later the programme was finally aired. The original sixty hours of film had been whittled down to barely ten minutes and bore little relationship to what had actually happened!

We were really disappointed and rather surprised at the very cynical stance the director had taken, one that bordered on ridicule. Most of that amazing week lay on the cutting room floor and the highly edited, fragmented impression that remained bore little resemblance to reality. It was a sobering reminder for me, anyway, that documentaries and news programmes can be tailored and trimmed to suit the whim, agenda, prejudices and preconceptions of the director.

We also learned from this experience how important it is not to be swayed by other people's perceptions, or to make rash judgments based on snapshots and soundbites, but to see the bigger picture. We can look back on the event now and conclude that the truth, like beauty, is very much in the eye of the beholder. What may appear as the truth may be only a tiny, distorted aspect of it.

Some time later a stranger came up to Linda and me while we were shopping at our local supermarket. Apparently, she recognised us from the TV programme. We hadn't realised that anyone had actually watched it. For a moment we didn't know whether to be embarrassed or proud, but by the smile on her face we felt like stars for a moment or two. She fell short of actually asking us for autographs but left looking distinctly happy, so we had our moment of fame.

Turning Points

"Hope for the best but expect the unexpected," said the wise monk in the classic TV drama *Kung-Fu*. But we could never have been prepared for the unexpected news that came out of the blue and hit us like a bombshell.

Our friend Eamon `phoned to tell us. We were stunned, speechless. We could hardly believe it. Gordon Higginson had passed away. A cold shiver ran down my spine as Eamon explained what had happened. It had all been very sudden. Gordon had been demonstrating at a local Spiritualist church when he had been taken ill; he had returned to his home in Longton and then passed peacefully during the night. It was no doubt the way he would have wanted.

We didn't know what to say. There was a stony silence as we searched for some suitable response but all we could feel was a sudden cold emptiness. We had lost a very dear and special friend. Gordon had been a wonderful friend and teacher for us as well as being a major inspiration along our spiritual path. We would really miss him, his warmth and humour as well as his amazing wisdom and knowledge;

still, we felt blessed and grateful for the times we had spent with him. Without doubt Gordon had been a very significant factor in the formation of our spiritual philosophy and understanding, which was to hold us in good stead for the future.

On subsequent visits to Stansted there was something missing. Gordon would always have been there at the door, smiling and warmly welcoming everyone. He exuded a presence and a quality that was hard to replace. His photograph still hangs proudly on the wall in the library, and no doubt he keeps a watchful eye over proceedings and continues his work in Spirit.

Sadly, to my knowledge, only one book has been written about Gordon's life[3] and there is no significant recorded or documented evidence of his wonderful work and words of wisdom. His lasting legacy, however, lives on in the impact he had on so many people during his lifetime.

He was an avid storyteller and one of his anecdotes gives a taste of the measure of the man. During WWII, Gordon oversaw a squad of soldiers; at one point they were stranded behind enemy lines in the pitch black, with no means of finding the right direction or any obvious avenue of escape. Behind them lay impenetrable darkness and in front of them the raging torrent of a river. They were trapped. Suddenly Gordon psychically saw a bouncing ball of spirit light guiding them to the shallowest point of the river and ultimately leading them to safety. Whilst at first his men may have scoffed and ridiculed his psychic gifts, from that moment on Gordon Higginson became the most popular company leader, his credentials never doubted again.

In civilian life, his gifts were exceptional. At his Longton church the turning of the year was often celebrated by a special service of communion with Spirit, at which Gordon would channel through deep trance a very high spirit guide and teacher known simply as Light.

---

[3] *On the Side of Angels* (J Bassett, SNU Publications, 1993).

Gordon spoke only rarely of these special events but it seems clear that he was accessing a very deep and profound level of spiritual teaching.

His enigmatic words to Linda and me so long before, however, continued to ring in our ears.

"I see you both working in America for Spirit, but not necessarily within Spiritualism. I see connections with America." We had wondered what exactly he meant, but were soon to find out.

The Chocolate Factory. I couldn't quite work out what chocolate had to do with metaphysics, but I was intrigued by the title of the talk and was curious to find out more. It was the final day of a new week-long course at Stansted called Living with the Power of Spirit, organised by Judith Seaman, a respected trance medium, spiritual teacher and Vice President of the SNU.

Judith was keen to develop spiritual thinking and remind us that we are Spirit here and now and that we can call upon the power of Spirit to enrich and enlighten our lives at any moment. We found Judith to be a breath of fresh air, a very enlightened soul who was honest enough to admit that "There is more to mediumship than messages." It became a fascinating few days, but little did we realise just how pivotal this particular talk would be on our spiritual journey.

The Chocolate Factory turned out to be a very clever metaphor for the subconscious mind. Judith made the talk fun with some carefully chosen drawings that illustrated the story of a chocolate factory, from the shop floor and production line up to Board Room level, each stage of the process representing an aspect of mind. When all the ingredients were right and everyone was working in total harmony of purpose, then the best results could be achieved – a perfect chocolate bar. There was another important element, however.

"Unless we ship out what we have produced for others to enjoy and benefit from," Judith explained, "there is no reward. Rewards only come when we deliver the finished product and receive money in return. In the metaphorical chocolate factory of the mind, the reward comes from sharing the knowledge we have gained and seeing others find a new direction in life. Many people go to many workshops but do nothing with what they learn, like making chocolate and just keeping it in the warehouse."

Similarly, she explained, when our thoughts, feelings, actions and intentions are in perfect alignment – when all of our ingredients are in order – then the instructions to our subconscious mind will help produce the results we desire in our lives, as long as we put what we have learned into practice.

"If you would like to know more," Judith suggested, "there's a really good book I would recommend by Raymond Charles Barker, called *The Invisible Self*. They may have a copy in the college bookshop. And if you are interested, this teaching is from what is called The Science of Mind."

This was the first time we had ever come across the name, but unbeknownst to us at the time The Science of Mind was destined to play a major part in our lives. It is curious, looking back, to discern how significant that lecture at Stansted was in our evolving spiritual education. But nothing happens by chance. It was all part of an unfolding pattern, a golden thread of divine synchronicity that was already weaving its magic in the tapestry of our lives. After the talk, Linda rushed to the bookshop to buy the last remaining copy of Barker's book, ostensibly as a belated birthday present for me. But I hardly got a look in. With typical enthusiasm, Linda spent the rest of the evening avidly reading every page.

"This is amazing stuff!" She devoured the contents and proceeded to give me a running commentary on the key points. We were hooked. This was just up our alley and resonated perfectly with everything we had always believed.

Judith later shared with us how, as a young girl, she had been terribly shy and lacking in self-confidence. A guiding voice from Spirit had over time helped her not only to overcome these problems but to become a much sought-after medium, teacher and public speaker, demonstrating to hundreds of people all over the country and ultimately rising to the heights of Vice President and then President of the SNU.

On reading a book about The Science of Mind she had been amazed to discover that the modern metaphysical teachings therein echoed almost precisely the words of wisdom and guidance she had received from Spirit and which had helped to change her life.

That talk, that book, that day changed our lives too.

Barker's book inspired us to do some further Sherlock Holmes-style investigations and Linda, being an ex-market research executive, relished the challenge. The first port of call was to contact the publishers, Fowlers. Bearing in mind the book was a fairly dated classic we wondered whether the publishers were still in business; they were, only just, and they told us that there had once been a Science of Mind church "somewhere near Bournemouth", but they doubted that it was still functioning.

After several 'phone calls (this was pre-Google) and some exhaustive enquiries, we finally located a name and number for the solitary Science of Mind centre in the UK. It was a shot in the dark. We dialled the number. There was no reply. We tried again and this time a polite but friendly voice answered with a distinct American accent.

"Hello, this is Science of Mind, UK. How can I help?"

It was our first encounter with the Reverend Rita Parr, Minister of the small but flourishing Science of Mind centre near Bournemouth. She was intrigued by our story of how we had discovered Science of

Mind and her church in the first place and cordially invited us to attend one of her Sunday services.

A couple of weeks later, we set off bright and early one sunny Sunday morning for the two-hour drive. Bournemouth, with its popular pier and promenade, long sandy beaches and temperate climate is colloquially known as The English Riviera. When temperatures soar it attracts hundreds of day trippers, tourists and holiday makers. We managed to miss the crowds and the traffic, bypassing the main thoroughfares and heading for Parkstone, then Poole and the Grasshopper Hotel, the venue for Science of Mind UK's Sunday services. We arrived with minutes to spare and walked up to the entrance where a small floor-standing sign boldly announced, Change your Thinking – Change your Life.

Like a proud mother hen watching over her brood, the Reverend Rita stood in the doorway and greeted us with a warm, welcoming smile and a slightly restrained Californian-style hug. Polite and poised, with a formality that was rather more English in nature than American, she was clearly well liked and respected in her closed community for her experience, learning and metaphysical wisdom.

There were about forty or more people present, congregating in a back room of the hotel. We mingled with the crowd, an eclectic mixture of young and old, mainly female, and a few colourful characters who instantly caught our eye. Several rows of seats were laid out in an orderly semicircle focused on a small raised dais with a well-worn wooden lectern, a vase of multi-coloured flowers and in the background an array of wall-mounted posters reminding us how to be 'healthy, wealthy and wise'.

We sat at the back to observe proceedings on this, our first visit, but Reverend Rita had other ideas and quickly announced us as her guests from London, following which, our cover blown, we were brought very much into the heart of proceedings. The atmosphere was friendly and relaxed and we immediately felt at home in the pseudo-ecclesiastical environment. There were just enough church-like touches to remind us that we were at a Sunday service, albeit far removed from a traditional one. The opening prayer/invocation was followed by some very unchurch-like affirmation songs that brought a smile to our faces, vigorous organ music being played with great gusto by the resident musician, a softly spoken meditation and an enlightening talk by Reverend Rita herself.

Towards the end of the service people were invited to share what were called 'demonstrations', personal testimonials to how Science of Mind had helped to heal and transform their lives. We found it at once comforting, quite profound and uplifting. The service concluded with a rousing rendition of *Let There be Peace on Earth, and Let it Begin with Me.* There was just time for a quick cup of herbal tea, a browse around the centre's bookstore and a few final words with one or two of the lingering congregants.

"Please come again," Reverend Rita invited us, as we made our way to the door. "You are always welcome."

As we returned to our car, clouds were already beginning to obscure the midday sun and there was a fine drizzle in the air, but the change in the weather did not dampen our mood. Beneath the apparent simplicity of the service I had detected something deep and meaningful. I was definitely drawn to this teaching that was so in keeping with what I had always thought, felt and believed. Indeed, we both felt instinctively that Science of Mind was somehow destined to play a significant part in our lives.

From that day on we attended Sunday services at the Bournemouth church whenever we could. There would always be a cordial welcome from Reverend Rita and gradually we got to know many regular members of the congregation. Among them, notably, was Dave G who was an NLP Master and a prolific author, metaphysician and inveterate manifester of Science of Mind teachings. He shared many inspiring stories of how he had used the principles to achieve success, happiness and prosperity in his own life. We learned a lot from Dave in those early days and spent several satisfying sessions in conversation with him and his lovely wife Sue at their home in Southampton. Dave really seemed to have got it.

"It's all about letting go of any attachment to the outcome," he would explain. "And when you truly let go, the things you most desire just come about – but don't seem so important anymore!"

We laughed at the apparent irony, but Dave had proved the efficacy of the principles in his own life. I for one could not wait to discover these mysterious principles for myself and see how we could apply them to our own lives. Yes, it all sounded a bit like magic, but it was the sort of magic I wanted to know more about.

"This stuff really works," Dave would tell us, wide-eyed with enthusiasm. Then he would add the magic words: "You must go to Asilomar!" We had no idea what he was talking about. But it was not the last time the name Asilomar would come up in conversation.

Change Your Thinking!

'What is Science of Mind all about?' I wondered, delving deeper into this purportedly life-changing philosophy. It wasn't science in the conventional sense (although the discoveries of quantum mechanics are apparently moving in a similar direction) and it certainly had nothing to do with Scientology. It was in fact the inspired creation of a visionary spiritual teacher in the early years of the twentieth century, and could be summed up in the simple but meaningful statement, 'Change your thinking, change your life.'

As my research deepened, I became fascinated by the sheer depth and scope of this man's work that spanned nearly half a century and over a hundred books. This, I thought, was no fleeting, fly by night ideology, but a profound and relevant philosophy. Linda and I had read widely on a range of spiritual subjects and were well versed in a variety of metaphysical studies; but Science of Mind seemed to offer a comprehensive and structured teaching that made sense to us and brought all the strands together. We had moved from New Age thinking to New Thought practice and for us, at least, it seemed like the perfect next step along our spiritual journey. It was another of life's invitations!

The Science of Mind (and Spirit, as it was originally known), was founded in America in the 1920s by Ernest Holmes, a visionary philosopher, healer, metaphysician and modern day mystic. It owed a certain homage to the works of Thomas Troward, a respected Scottish judge and a man of great virtue and intellect, and grew out of the burgeoning New Thought Movement in the nineteenth century. Here was a teaching that not only stimulated and nourished the heart and mind but offered practical and positive spiritual tools to apply to everyday life.

Fundamentally, it speaks to 'Oneness, the unity of all life, the creative power of thought and a Power for Good that we call God.' The more I learned, the more impressed I was by the man, the message and the meaning encapsulated in this pronouncement, uniquely associated with Ernest Holmes:

'There is a power for good in the universe
that is greater than we are,
that we can use.'

It is surprising that Science of Mind had never really taken root in the UK, although the philosophy has been espoused by many modern spiritual teachers from Wayne Dyer to Louise Hay, probably one of the best known exponents and who, unknown to many, actually herself became a Science of Mind practitioner and minister.

This philosophy is an amalgam of ancient wisdom and essential truths gleaned from the great religions and faiths of both East and West. It began life as a structured teaching for 'positive living' but grew rapidly in popularity and eventually evolved into an organisation that spanned the whole of the United States. Nowadays there are hundreds of churches and spiritual centres with hundreds of thousands of students worldwide.

Whilst in its early days the terminology tended to be pseudo-religious, with ministers, churches and Sunday services (although the content was far removed from conventional religion), in more recent times books like *The Secret* and popular interest in the 'law of attraction' reflect a more modern interpretation of the teachings and the key principle, 'It is done unto you as you believe.'

We were attracted by its open-minded, non-dogmatic approach that empowers the individual to take responsibility for their own life. From the springboard of Spiritualism we were discovering a philosophy that fitted us like a glove and reflected an even wider outlook on God, life and the power of thought. We were eager to find out more and it would not be long before the next few pieces of the jigsaw would begin to fit together.

Reverend Rita, keen to spread the word, had organised a series of one-day and weekend seminars and had invited Dr Mark Vierra from Los Angeles, California, to headline the programme.

"You two must come," she implored us, "and you will just love Dr Mark."

Dr Mark was indeed a charismatic, larger than life character, the sort you might expect to see in a Hollywood movie. He was the Senior Minister and Spiritual Leader of the North Hollywood Center for Spiritual Living, a thriving community on the fringe of Los Angeles. His sense of humour, unbounding energy and rich, honeyed tone of voice (he could have been an actor) had earned him high standing in the Movement. He had become a very popular and much sought-after speaker – and here he was, headlining the first summer seminar for the Bournemouth Centre.

There was a terrific turnout with nearly a hundred people present on a beautifully sunny July weekend at the Durley Hall, a friendly modern hotel on Bournemouth's West Cliff. We had travelled direct from London and the seminar room was already packed to capacity when we arrived. We just managed to find some seats right at the back. Dr Mark's towering presence – he was as big in stature as he was in personality – filled the room and embraced everyone in it.

He talked about God, not as a detached and distant deity but as Spirit up close and personal. He talked about abundance, meaning not simply money but also health, relationships and a more fulfilled way of living. Especially, he urged us to raise our consciousness in order to avail ourselves of the limitless supply of good in the universe: if we wish to manifest more good in our lives, we need to bring it into our realm of experience.

Mark Vierra was dramatic and entertaining and he captured the audience with his charm and humour. What impressed us most, however, was his no-nonsense honesty and candour and down-to-earth approach. He made Science of Mind accessible and spirituality seem like fun! And he addressed life's ups and downs and the inevitable challenges that face us all.

"We may walk through the valley of the shadow," he intoned in a deep, serious Hollywood drawl, "but we don't have to pitch our tent there."

Amidst the laughter that followed we recognised a serious point. Yes, we all face problems and challenges but we don't have to let them define us or become our life story.

Mark concluded his talk with a beautiful, flowing meditation for peace, health and prosperity. Then, as the afternoon drew to a close, we managed a few private words with him. His warmth, humour and enthusiasm were infectious and we felt like kindred spirits. Little did we realise how instrumental he would be in the unfolding of our spiritual path.

"If you guys come to LA you must visit my church," he suggested purposefully. Then came the punch line. "And you must come to Asilomar!"

There it was again, the magic word. We still had no idea what or where this intriguing place called Asilomar was or what significance it might have in the grand scheme of things. All that he (and Dave) would say was, "It is an experience – and you must experience it for yourself."

In the summer of 1998, seemingly out of the blue, an opportunity presented itself. A project we had been working on had come to completion and a holiday we had been planning failed to materialise, so we thought, 'Well, let's go to Asilomar.' We had no idea where to begin, but the idea would not go away and begged us to take it further. It would be a shift from our normal holiday routine, a pleasant but predictable pattern of summers in Mallorca, long breaks in the sun reading, writing and looking out onto the azure blue of the ocean in an idyllic Balearic bay. But this new idea promised an adventure into the unknown. And what an adventure it would turn out to be...

We sat back in our seats on the British Airways Jumbo Jet bound for San Francisco, California, USA, after a few hectic weeks of planning and preparation. There had been flights to book and hotels to arrange, regulations to check and registrations made, maps and timetables to peruse and a host of other details to see to. Flying high above the clouds, a sea of fluffy white beneath us and the deep blue sky stretching as far as the eye could see, with the hypnotic hum of the giant jet's engines in the background, we felt immersed in a wonderful, dreamy sense of peace and anticipation of an extraordinary adventure. After an eleven-hour flight skirting the coast of Canada and North America, we descended through the clouds to catch our first glimpse of the Golden Gate city, the tall skyscrapers glinting gold in the afternoon sunlight.

We marched through the arrivals lounge and security, collected our luggage and hailed one of those iconic yellow cabs to a local motel for the night. We would have to be up and out early the next morning to catch the Greyhound bus that would take us all the way down the coastal highway for the five-hour journey to Monterey, Pacific Grove and onwards. Despite the jetlag we slept well, woke early and enjoyed a healthy American-style breakfast before heading out in the grey dawn to the bus terminal. The city was still asleep. There would be no time for sightseeing: Fisherman's Wharf and Pier 39 would have to wait.

On the crowded bus we were wedged between early morning commuters and casual weekend travellers. We left the environs of San Francisco as the morning mists began to clear to reveal a perfectly clear blue sky. The journey took us down the Pacific coastal highway, picking up and dropping off passengers along the way from San Jose to Monterey, and gradually the numbers dwindled until by the time we arrived at Pacific Grove we were the only passengers left.

"Where's you going?" enquired our driver with a friendly smile and a deep, languid southern accent. When we mentioned Asilomar her eyes lit up. "Well, sure, I'll take you there." She meant right to the door and proceeded to turn the bus around, right off her designated route, and kindly chauffeured us all the way into Asilomar itself.

We passed through the picturesque towns of Monterey, Carmel (where Clint Eastwood had once been Mayor) and Pacific Grove before tackling the winding, wooded road that led up to Asilomar. Already we could sense a different atmosphere. The air was cooler and fresher, the traffic lighter and quieter and in the background was the soothing sound of the ocean. We felt altogether nearer to nature. The bus turned a corner…

Asilomar was like nothing we had ever experienced before, more like a nature reserve than a conference centre, with its sprawling complex of wood and brick chalet-style buildings and tree-lined walkways. The bus stopped right outside Reception so we thanked our very helpful driver and took our first deep, revitalising breaths of the Bay air. As we stood in line to check in we felt an encroaching sense of tiredness. We had done so much in the last twenty-four hours we hardly knew what day it was. But we were so happy to be here at last and, strangely enough, it reminded us of the first time we had visited Stansted – again, it felt like we were coming home.

Words can hardly convey the sheer rugged beauty and magical energy of this extraordinary place and we now understood what Dave and Dr Mark had meant when they said, "It has to be experienced!" To be on a spiritual retreat in such a beautiful, unique and peaceful setting with hundreds of like minds and some of the finest teachers in the field was an absolute blessing.

The name Asilomar, in Spanish, means 'refuge by the sea' and it had been the brainchild of a visionary American architect over a century ago, who carved a breathtaking spiritual centre into the sand dunes and rugged coastline of north California. It became known as a place of outstanding natural beauty and peace and has attracted interest from a wide variety of organisations, both religious and secular. Asilomar has been the iconic venue for Science of Mind conferences since the 1960s, the idyllic setting a perfect backdrop to the evolving teachings and attracting many of the most eminent New Thought leaders including Ernest Holmes himself.

The rustic, wooden and stone buildings that form the hub of the complex were arranged in an irregular format sympathetic to the environment, each with a unique style and character, perfectly reflecting the message and awareness of the divine presence in all things. Close to nature with the gentle murmur of the ocean in the background and a light breeze shifting the ever-changing landscape of heather-covered dunes, this really is a 'refuge by the sea'.

Having collected our keys, a programme for the week and a site map, we set off to our lodgings, a bright and airy first floor apartment with wide windows overlooking Merrill Hall, the conference centre, theatre and centre of the community. We were fortunate as many of the apartments were spread out all over the sprawling complex, several minutes' walk from the centre of things. But nobody seemed to mind, there was an easy-going, unrushed atmosphere.

Merrill Hall is the very heart of the complex, perched high on a mound surrounded by trees and dominating the nearby landscape. It is indeed an impressive piece of architecture and had weathered the passing years with little signs of ageing. The high, vaulted wooden roof, replete with immaculate carvings and the wide yawning auditorium, offered a great sense of space. But as we entered the hall – having been thoroughly hugged by well-wishers, a curiously Californian protocol – we encountered a teeming mass of humanity; there must have been at least eight or nine hundred people present and barely a seat to spare. Vibrant music reverberated through the rafters and people got up from their seats to sway to the insistent rhythms (the music was exceptional). We managed to find a couple of seats but before we had time to peruse the evening programme a friendly neighbour approached, no doubt recognising a couple of newbies.

"Hi guys, where are you from? Is this your first time here?" We realised that despite the popularity of Asilomar in the United States, overseas visitors were few and far between and we began to feel like celebrities. "We just love your British accent!" By the end of the evening we had made dozens of new friends.

The talks were lively and thought-provoking, some serious and profound, others personal, poetic and humorous; but all were entertaining and enlightening, enhanced by beautiful soul-stirring music. As the evening drew to a close, we had enjoyed a feast of metaphysical magic. If the rest of the week was anything like this, we thought, we were in for a treat and we somehow sensed that something extra special was going to happen.

How do they manage to feed so many people, so well and so quickly? Sitting round a table with eight or ten new faces, dining on wholesome soups, salads and savouries, was a wonderful way to make new friends and discover some of the deeper secrets and stories of

Asilomar. For many people, we found, this retreat was the highlight of their year, an opportunity to catch up with old friends and experience some of the finest speakers in the movement. If only, we mused, there was something like this back home in the UK...

The week was a whirlwind of activity yet we still found time to walk along the beach and catch the energy of the ocean, to meet and share stories with fascinating people, to enjoy the welcome warmth of the midday sun and the cool, crisp evening air. At night, raccoons would emerge from their lairs wide-eyed and distinctive in their black and white coats, while during the day deer roamed freely around the grounds or sauntered through the dunes to turn up unexpectedly at the back door of one's apartment. In the early mornings, sea mists would sweep in to blanket everything in a damp chill. Afternoons would see people lounging on the decking outside the community centre to catch precious rays of sunshine. And the evenings were magical, with music, moonlight and a star-studded nightscape.

The theme of this week was We Grow in Joy. Linda and I both felt that we were indeed growing and new vistas of opportunity were opening up for us. But it was something that happened on the final day of the conference that really made an impact on us.

Jo Pirello was an affable, ebullient Italian American whose Personal Expression Workshop had become legendary at Asilomar and were a must for all newcomers to attend. His New York charm and forthright manner quickly won us over and enticed us to go along on the final Friday afternoon. It sounded fun, something different, we thought, perhaps lighter fare to round off the week: a sort of *Asilomar Has Talent*. But the reality, we discovered, was far from frivolous.

Jo and his crew had established themselves in a roomy, ranch-style chalet at the far end of the complex and had invited a group of willing guests to share their gifts. There was a diverse menu of talent that afternoon: singers and songwriters, dancers, drummers, actors, artists and poets, an impressive display of the creative process in action. Then it was our turn. And we had come to the impromptu session without any planning, preparation or props.

We had fifteen minutes to explain and demonstrate a taste of our healing meditation and colour workshop. It was a tall order but we quickly got in the zone and produced an impromptu version of what we do back home, all done at a breathless pace. We managed to conjure up some suitable music for a brief guided meditation, which went down better than expected; Linda gave a short talk about the language of colour and then proceeded to give a few spontaneous colour readings that were warmly received. Then we concluded the session with our Healing Fountain, surprising ourselves by just how much we had been able to squeeze into those few fleeting minutes.

"That was great!" said Jo enthusiastically. Then he added, "Why don't you submit a workshop proposal for next year?" We were taken aback. It had been the last thing on our minds, but the seed had now been planted and we promised to follow it up when we returned home.

Before we knew it, the week was over. It had been an incredible experience that would take us time to digest fully. Our minds were buzzing with possibilities as we headed to Reception to catch a taxi for the half-hour journey to Carmel, where we planned to spend a few days relaxing and enjoying some more real Californian sunshine.

Carmel is small, charming and intimate and has more in common with European café culture and architecture than Los Angeles or San Francisco. With its high-class shops and glossy bars, boutiques, bistros and Mediterranean-style open air cafés, we spent a pleasant, peaceful and relaxing few days there to round off an amazing holiday experience. The small but quaint Normandy Hotel was bedecked with festoons of brightly coloured flowers and hanging baskets, set amidst a rustic open air shopping mall. We were surrounded by vibrant colours, music and beautiful sunshine and it felt more like a Caribbean resort as we spent our time sightseeing, sunbathing or just sitting and chatting on the veranda, lunching on delicious fresh fruit salad and creamy Californian cottage cheese.

New Birth

On the flight back to London we had books to read, plenty to think about and sleep to catch up on. There was that strange spaced out feeling of jetlag and the after-effects of extraordinary new experiences. Once home, it took us a while to settle back into normality and routine before we found time to knuckle down and prepare a proposal for a colour healing and meditation workshop. The prospect of returning to Asilomar was hugely appealing, though frankly we were sceptical of our chances; after all, we were virtual novices in a field of experienced Science of Mind practitioners.

Nevertheless, we applied ourselves with energy and enthusiasm and before long had the makings of a punchy, interesting and unique proposal that certainly stirred our own imagination and, we hoped, might arouse similar interest at the home office in Los Angeles. Ceremoniously, we stamped and sealed a large white envelope addressed to the Planning Committee and, with a prayer for a positive outcome, slipped it into the post box. The deed was done, we had let go and let God, and to all intents and purposes we then forgot all about it.

But a few months later, an air mail envelope bearing the distinctive marks of the Science of Mind organisation arrived. Linda rushed upstairs excitedly to show me and we held our breath as she gingerly opened it. We read the words over and over to make sure we had got it right: 'The Asilomar Planning Committee is pleased to invite Linda and David Serlin to present their workshop Expressions of Spirit through the Power of Colour...' Our proposal had been accepted. It was a dream come true and we were on our way back to LA.

We couldn't help but recall Gordon Higginson's prophecy years before. "I see you both working in America for Spirit, but not necessarily within Spiritualism." Our first instinct was to feel rather daunted, after all we were novices in all this. But then we remembered our mantra: if life (Spirit) offers you a golden opportunity, you have to say "Yes!"

The invitation was for the whole two weeks of the Asilomar conference, with a weekend off in between. We would have to cover our own fares and accommodation but would receive complimentary conference registrations, worth hundreds of dollars. It was not this that persuaded us, it was just such an honour and privilege to be invited and we were absolutely thrilled.

Over the ensuing months, we created, planned and rehearsed a detailed workshop programme, something unique and fun yet insightful. We invented innovative processes, devised a series of guided meditations and timed everything to the second, leaving no stone unturned.

Linda had conceived her own original interpretation of the language of colour and assembled an array of vibrantly coloured scarves, ribbons and feathers, aura images, pictures and chakra charts and, leaving nothing to chance, had put her ideas to the test with a few well received dress rehearsals. I confess that I was impressed by her motivation and enthusiasm and I learned a lot about colour myself. On one level, the workshops were informative and entertaining, but there was something more; somehow, a pathway had opened to something deeper, more meaningful and profound. People were stunned by the personal revelations and insights they provided and there was no doubt that Spirit was guiding and inspiring Linda to an ever higher level of intuitive wisdom. We worked well as a team, each contributing our particular talents and expertise, and really enjoyed moulding the final shape of the work.

Before we knew it, we were standing in line at the Virgin Atlantic check-in desk at Heathrow Airport. This time we planned to fly direct to LA, stay overnight at a nearby hotel and catch the early morning shuttle flight to the tiny provincial airport at Monterey. By now we knew the routine. We settled into our snug seats and wondered how many films one could watch during an eleven-hour flight; but after two blockbusters and the effects of several days' hectic preparations, sleep soon took over.

We collected our cases, joined a lengthy queue for Customs and Security and eventually emerged into dazzling LA Saturday afternoon sunshine – though our body clocks were still hovering around early morning Sunday UK time – to be engulfed by a blanket of heat, the urgent honking of car horns and the hustle of hundreds of passengers all hailing cabs or waiting for pick-ups. A quick snack at the hotel and then we retired gracefully into a luxurious king size bed and enjoyed several hours of peaceful, uninterrupted slumber until dawn broke. Tinges of orange and red etched the morning sky as Los Angeles stirred into life. The hotel shuttle bus ferried us back to the airport, where we grabbed a quick breakfast before checking in for the early morning flight to Monterey in a tiny twin-engine Aero Jet, capacity thirty-two and top speed a modest two hundred miles an hour.

The scenery along the way was stunning; we had a bird's eye view of mountains and gorges, valleys and forests and the winding Pacific Highway that snaked its way north from Los Angeles. It was a breathtakingly beautiful landscape unlike anything we had ever seen before, the vivid blue of the Pacific Ocean contrasting with the changing colours of the countryside, mustard yellows, verdant lush greens and the golden amber of heather covering the hills. The journey was an experience in itself.

Monterey Provincial Airport has a tiny terminal building and just one luggage conveyor belt. We suspected that one or two of our fellow travellers were also destined for Asilomar and we wondered what their stories were, what had brought them to this extraordinary place. Our taxi headed purposefully onto the motorway for the relatively short journey to Asilomar where the roads and wooded, hilly landscape seemed pleasantly familiar.

Now recognised as staff, we had been allocated a privileged location deep in the complex with a stunning view of the ocean and dunes. Quickly unpacking, we freshened up and rushed off to our first meeting for workshop facilitators where we were handed our programme for the conference. There was a pretty hefty schedule with four ninety-minute workshops each week. But we were up for the challenge.

Expressions of Spirit through the Power of Colour

An inspiring and enlightening workshop experience
using guided meditation, various colour processes
and group healing situations to help discover our true potential
and explore our individual relationship with the spirit of colour.
The aim of the workshop, apart from being fun, informative
and uplifting, is to give every participant a new and deeper awareness
and understanding of colour, its relevance in our life as an expression
of the divine Spirit and how it can benefit us
practically, physically, emotionally and spiritually.

Unusually for Asilomar, temperatures hit the mid-seventies and for much of the time we were working in shirtsleeves in almost heatwave conditions. Far from putting people off, however, it seemed to create a happy, holiday atmosphere. And despite being the new kids on the block we had already attracted a band of loyal followers, among them a garrulous young man from San Francisco who, having attended one of our workshops, avidly set about promoting our cause, spreading the word and recruiting people from all over the campus. By the end of the first week attendances had rocketed, the venues packed to capacity with standing room only and people leaning in over opened windows to catch a glimpse of proceedings. It was bizarre and gratifying to receive such an enthusiastic response. Clearly the language of colour appealed to even more people than we had anticipated, perhaps because it was original, appealed to the heart as well as to the mind, and above all was fun!

During the course of our workshops some extraordinary manifestations took place. Standing at the back of the room, keeping to herself and quietly observing proceedings, a young woman stepped forward to take part in the healing fountain meditation at the end of the session. She looked incredibly pale and frail and was very unsteady on her feet. Later, she explained that she had been ill for some time but had felt 'impelled' to attend our workshop. During the healing she had felt a sudden surge of energy and the colour returning to her face. "It was wonderful," she told us. Amazingly, her weakness and fatigue had just disappeared.

"Now, what do you think of this?" Two very animated ladies from southern California confronted us after one workshop and thrust their notebooks into our hands. They had been sitting at different ends of the room, busily scribbling notes, when they had both observed something very peculiar. One lady had been writing in black ink while the other, her new-found friend, had been writing equally voluminous notes in blue. Suddenly, and with no apparent explanation, the black ink had turned blue and the blue ink had turned black! It was quite bizarre, a psychic phenomenon produced by the energy in the room, perhaps, or was it just Spirit's way of bringing together two souls who clearly had a lot in common?

Coloured ribbon readings had become an increasingly popular feature of the programme. By the combination of colours chosen, Linda would give an intuitive reading providing fascinating and at times uncannily profound insights into a person's life path and potential. There was never any shortage of volunteers. On one occasion Linda felt drawn to a lady sitting on a table at the back of the room (we had run out of chairs).

"I feel particularly attracted to this lady," she began. "You have a presence about you and straight away I can see you surrounded by books and papers, important documents." The woman listened intently to Linda's analysis. "I see a lot of brown around you and other colours that suggest study, qualifications and – dare I say – promotion to high office of some sort."

Unbeknownst to Linda, that woman turned out to be Dr Kathy Hearn, a highly regarded Science of Mind minister and soon to be elected Community Spiritual Leader (President) of the Science of Mind Organisation, a post she was to hold for several years. Dr Kathy became a good friend and was very supportive of our later ventures to promote the philosophy in the UK, although at the time we didn't have the faintest inkling of that possibility.

By the end of the first week we were ready for a break. The unseasonably hot weather had continued (Asilomar is situated in a bay renowned for its chilly, damp clime). We spent the weekend lazing by the pool or walking along the beach, watching the cormorants and herring gulls dart and weave and the surfers expertly skimming the giant, foaming waves. We became absorbed by the unique energy and atmosphere of Asilomar, the people, the place and its sheer rugged beauty, and finally realised what people had meant by 'the Asilomar experience'. Being there in its energy, one really gets what it's all about and can sense the full magic of this extraordinary place. And there is only one thing better than a week at Asilomar – two weeks.

We had been bowled over by the supportive response to our workshops and had also used our free time well, attending as many talks and activities as we could fit in. When we weren't listening or dancing to the music, we would be sharing others' interesting stories and experiences, staying up late chatting with newfound friends until we were too tired to talk anymore.

But whilst we felt blessed to be in such a stimulating and meaningful environment, with interesting and inspiring, like-minded people, we knew that the time would soon come to leave. The nagging question at the back of our minds was, 'How can we take some of this magic home with us? Where do we go from here?'

No sooner had the thought been formed than the law of attraction kicked in and we received an interesting and unexpected reply from the universe. An American couple who had attended one of our workshops approached us with a special request: they were due to relocate to London for their work and were keen to stay connected to Science of Mind people in the UK.

Suddenly we had the inspired idea to start our own Science of Mind study group. It seemed obvious and natural, and before we had time for second thoughts we had recruited our first two members. We had no idea what was involved, but such was the power of Asilomar that we felt up for anything.

Finally, we headed back to Monterey to spend a few days reflecting on our amazing Asilomar experience before returning home to London. The Monterey Beach Hotel was our home for the next few days, perfectly located right on the beach so we could literally step out of our ground floor bedroom suite onto the white, silky soft sand. At night we dined by candlelight on fresh Pacific salmon and garden vegetables while looking out to sea and, if we were lucky, catching a glimpse in the distance of dolphins dancing in the moonlight. After a few lovely days in Monterey, sampling the trendy harbour-side restaurants, artisan shops and galleries, we were ready to make our way back to London.

It had been an idyllic couple of weeks and our heads were still in the clouds when we arrived home, our thoughts already turning to our newly conceived Science of Mind study group and to the fast approaching new millennium. What would the new century bring? Much as our visits to Stansted had been, we sensed that the Asilomar experiences would become an important and integral part of our lives.

We took our first steps on what was to be an extraordinary new spiritual journey in August, 1999, when the Kings Langley Science of Mind study group was formed.

The new millennium dawned with a fanfare of fireworks and spectacular celebrations, full of promise, high hopes and a few (unfounded) fears. The sun still set, the birds still sang and life went on much as before. Our little study group gradually grew and we looked forward eagerly to our Sunday afternoon meetings, which soon became the highlight of the week. We experimented with affirmations, music and meditations, there was a lot of fun and laughter, and our numbers increased as we explored the deeper realms and meaning of metaphysics.

With the birth of our son, life took on a whole new meaning and focus. Overseas trips would have to be shelved for a while as other priorities loomed and it was a time of rapid change and growth on all fronts. Our study group was expanding and we continued to practise the principles as best we could, becoming quite adept at spiritual mind treatments (a form of affirmative prayer). We promised ourselves that when our son was old enough we would take him with us to experience the magic of Asilomar for himself. It would be six years before that opportunity arose.

The journey, naturally, was slightly more complex now and we had to keep a watchful eye on our son, but he seemed to enjoy the rigours of travel. He loved the movies on the Virgin flight and revelled in the bouncy progress of the twin-engine jet that flew us to Monterey. Once at Asilomar, the kids' camp totally absorbed his time and energies and left us free to enjoy the conference.

Each time we had visited Asilomar so far, something special had happened on our return to the UK. Firstly, our workshop proposal had been accepted and secondly our study group had been conceived. So when, after quite a long absence, we visited for the third time, we wondered what magic lay in store. The theme for the week was Going Deeper. In the intervening years we had deepened and broadened our understanding of Science of Mind and already we could feel a change in tone and content as if we had moved on to an altogether deeper spiritual level.

"Something's calling me," sang Jami Lula, a charismatic musician with a voice like velvet and a guitar sound that sent shivers down the spine. "A little bit deeper than I've ever been before…" The music at Asilomar was always exceptional and so too was the quality and variety of the speakers. A young newly fledged minister from Chicago, Mark Anthony Lord, caught our attention. He was fun, exuberant and literally danced onto the stage. Yet it was actually something that happened over dinner on the last night that sent ripples – actually more like shock waves – to shift us further and deeper than we'd ever been before.

As we sat down, we were joined by Dr Mark Vierra and Dr Roger Juline, both experienced speakers and highly respected within the movement. During the course of conversation, we shared our thoughts and feelings about the week and our frustration that there was nothing like Asilomar in the UK.

"We could really do with a mini-Asilomar in England," said Linda wistfully. "Maybe somebody will get something together sometime?"

It was wishful thinking aimed at no-one in particular. There was silence. Then we noticed that both Mark and Roger were staring at us, smiling politely. There was a hiatus in the conversation, a kind of prescience in the air, and then a strange thought hit us.

"You don't mean us?" I uttered, shocked.

"Well, you are 'somebody'. What are you waiting for?" replied Mark with a smile. Before we had even digested that idea, he added, "If you set something up in England, I'll come over and do a talk or workshop for you and I'll support you in whatever way I can."

We were taken aback, even slightly overawed, but as the evening progressed the idea became increasingly attractive and feasible. Mark had already envisioned a trip to Europe and this way he could combine the two projects, whilst by the end of the evening Dr Roger, who was quite influential within the movement, was also already checking out ways he might be able to help us get our virgin project off the ground.

The rest of the evening was a flurry of excitement and, before we had time to stand back and reflect on what on Earth we had committed ourselves to, the seed had been planted and the word was out. What had begun as a simple, modest idea – maybe a one-day seminar – was beginning to build a momentum all of its own. We don't know quite how it happened but now we were getting offers of support from all sides. Mentioning our plans to Mark Anthony Lord, the dynamic young speaker from Chicago, he jumped at the opportunity.

"Just give me the date, I'd love to come too."

Even Jami Lula, the charismatic musician, got wind of the project and keenly volunteered his services. We were overwhelmed. For a start, we had no idea of how, where and when; we had no funds and just a small study group and a handful of interested friends back in the UK. It would be a giant leap of faith, yet we were determined to see it through; and with Spirit's help we knew anything was possible. For the next week or so, however, we put our plans on hold while we enjoyed the rest of our American vacation.

After the conference, we enjoyed a few days in carefree, laid-back Santa Monica. Situated on the sunny, southern Californian coastline and on the fringe of LA, with its long stretches of flat sandy beaches, iconic landmark pier and Ferris wheel (often featured in Hollywood movies), and with fabulous shops and restaurants on Third Street promenade, it offered the perfect, relaxing break.

Loewy's Hotel is right on the sea front and we spent idyllic mornings on long, leisurely walks or bike rides along the palm-fringed sidewalks that bordered the beach, pausing every now and again to bathe in the glorious sunshine or watch the yoga, Tai Chi and gravity-defying gymnasts performing their hair-raising stunts. Morning adventures often took us to nearby Venice (Muscle) Beach with its remnants of psychedelic art and graffiti, a throwback to the `Sixties, where long-haired, aged hippies manned stalls selling homemade jewellery, exotic paintings and garishly coloured tee-shirts with clever, good-humoured slogans. Buskers sang on street corners while body builders cavorted and performed their conspicuous morning routines in open air gyms. Finding our way back to the hotel, we skirted joggers, power walkers, rollerbladers and expert skateboarders. It was summer, it was fun, it was California where anything goes – and we loved it.

Oddly enough, Santa Monica and more specifically Venice Beach had been home to Ernest Holmes in his early years, while he was doing his research and writing, developing his ideas and the philosophy of Science of Mind. He too had been captivated by the warmth, the sunshine and relaxed Californian lifestyle and the open-minded attitudes that welcomed his teachings and provided the inspiration for some of his greatest work. We hoped that some of that inspiration would rub off on us too, as we contemplated the exciting days ahead and the new adventure we were embarking upon.

Keeping a promise we had made to our son, we then headed to Anaheim, Orange County, to the home of Disneyland. As we drove inland away from the coast, temperatures soared and the landscape changed. Far from the urban sprawl of Los Angeles, Anaheim gave a more sedate and orderly impression with its neatly laid out roads and streets.

But this was deceptive, for immediately we walked through the gates of Disneyland and queued for our badges, tickets and programmes, we became enmeshed in an amazing atmosphere of sheer fun. Apart from being brilliantly organised, handling thousands of visitors each day from all over the world, everyone seemed so joyful, staff and visitors alike. It certainly lived up to its reputation. Some of the rides were a bit scary but our youngster thoroughly enjoyed himself and we loved the energy and atmosphere of this fairy tale, fantasy, magical dreamland. We even returned in the evening to experience the highly vaunted fireworks display, a spectacular event with glittering figures from the Disney classics flying seamlessly across the night sky to a stunning musical score as an explosive symphony of colour and light lit up the whole arena.

Although a highly successful and commercial venture, there was something almost spiritual about the place in the way that so many people from so many different cultures and backgrounds all came together to celebrate happiness, fun and joy in such a relaxed and harmonious way. Walt Disney had been a man with a vision and, despite all the odds and constant opposition, he had persevered and seen his dream come to fruition.

We spent the remaining few days of our holiday relaxing by the pool. Home seemed a long way away, but we were looking forward to getting back and getting started on our new project, our vision of a mini-Asilomar in England. It seemed a distant dream but, as we had learned at Disneyland, dreams do come true.

Asilomar

Ernest Holmes

A Leap of Faith

To begin with, the plan was for a relatively modest affair: a village hall perhaps, a community centre or even a large room in a restaurant might be suitable. But somehow, as we embarked on a series of visits to local venues, 'small' just did not feel right. Our greater vision, if we were honest, was for something much grander befitting the subject, even though we were not quite sure exactly what that entailed yet. It required something outstanding that would make a real difference.

Gradually the search widened to include small hotels and halls, but still nothing seemed to fit the bill, being either too big or too small, too costly or just not available. Our sights were set on a date in late June or early July, before the school summer holidays and when the weather would hopefully be more clement. The right location was of paramount importance yet seemed elusive and despite our best endeavours we seemed to be going round in circles.

So we sat down and applied what we had learned by treating – creating a powerful positive affirmation – for what we wanted: the perfect venue to serve all our needs in a desirable location and at a sensible price. Then we waited… and Linda soon had an inspired idea.

"Why not try the Rudolf Steiner School in Kings Langley?" she suggested. "It has a beautiful theatre, dining room and lovely outdoor space and gardens. David, I think it will be perfect." It was actually right on our doorstep yet had been the last place on our minds. It was well located with ample parking and a theatre that could accommodate, optimistically, hundreds of people. It was worth a try and we wondered why we hadn't thought of it before. We called the school and made an appointment to see Dan, the Events Manager.

As soon we stepped into the spacious theatre we knew that it was just what we needed. There was a large stage, several rows of tiered seating and, most importantly, it had that 'something special' feeling about it. Dan showed us around the kitchen and dining area and a large adjoining room that would be ideal for a breakout workshop space. But how much would it cost and would it be available for when we needed it? The theatre was often used by the school itself and there were several regular outside organisations who booked the theatre well in advance; Dan promised to check the schedules and get back to us as soon as possible.

We waited patiently as the days passed, keeping our spirits up, until at last the 'phone call came. It was great news. The theatre was available for just the Saturday we had earmarked at the end of June and, should we want it, for a nominal extra charge we could have it for the whole weekend. Here was another invitation from the universe. We had never really considered a whole weekend event that would really be pushing the boat out and posing a whole set of new questions. But it sounded so good that we felt inspired to say, "Yes, let's go for it!"

The Steiner staff were so helpful and obliging, and the whole philosophy of their movement seemed completely compatible with what we were planning. Before we knew it, our modest one-day seminar had become a weekend event – and was soon to evolve into a full-blown international conference.

"Think big, aim high," we said to each other, like a rallying call from an Antony Robbins motivational seminar. (As it happens, I had just been listening to one of his very inspiring tapes.) And now, overnight, our aspirations and ambitions had rocketed and we needed to catch our breath. Yes, the prospect was really exciting, but also a giant leap of faith.

The next step was to invite a top-notch team of speakers and heading the list was Dr Mark Vierra so we called him at his Center in north Hollywood and updated him on our progress. He was delighted by the news, confirmed the dates had already been earmarked in his diary, and even suggested a title and theme for the event: The First UK Conference for Abundant Living. Little did we realise that, moreover, this was to be the first ever Science of Mind conference in the UK.

Word spread quickly that Mark, a widely respected and hugely popular speaker, had enlisted and was committed to our cause. So when we contacted Mark Anthony Lord in Chicago he too jumped at the opportunity, Jami Lula readily agreed to head our music team and Dr Kathy Hearn, now Community Spiritual Leader, joyfully accepted our invitation. Over in San Clemente, California, Dr Roger Juline kept his word by energetically promoting our case. What we did not know was that he was an influential member of the Hefferlin Foundation, a charitable organisation whose principal remit was to offer financial support to new ventures promoting the principles of Science of Mind worldwide. It hadn't even occurred to us that such grants might be available, and we were over the moon when Roger confirmed that we might be eligible; in fact, he went even further and suggested that Hefferlin might hold their next annual meeting in London to coincide with our conference. We had no funds ourselves so duly submitted a detailed budget forecast to the Foundation and their response exceeded all expectations. With the extra funding assured, we could now move ahead with our plans at full speed.

We set up a small organising committee with Linda and myself as co-chairs but in reality – isn't it always the way? – we ended up doing most of the work ourselves. Day by day we were also receiving applications and enquiries from potential speakers and musicians who relished the idea of being part of the first UK Conference. Sample CDs and CVs poured in but we had to be very discriminating as we only had one weekend to fill.

Still, however passionate and highly motivated we were, we did not have ITC skills; so when a friend offered to set up a website for us, we gratefully accepted and *www.abundantliving.co.uk* was born.

By early 2007 we had assembled a terrific team of speakers and musicians including, as well as those mentioned, Diane Harmony (author of the bestselling *Five Gifts for an Abundant Life*), Dr Marilyn Leo and Dr Tom Sannar (both acknowledged experts on the life of Ernest Holmes) and a colourful character from Holland called Corey Van Loon. A friend recommended Mark Hughes, a UK-based singer songwriter, who proved a great asset to our music team. And that, we thought, was it.

Like an intriguing jigsaw, the whole process was beginning to piece together. Whenever we needed someone or something and gave it our focus and attention, it seemed to manifest miraculously. They say that if we take the first step, Spirit will follow to make our way smooth and good. Well, we had taken a giant leap of faith and, looking back, there is no doubt that Spirit was guiding and inspiring us along the way.

Every now and again, Linda and I would step back from the whirl of activity and retreat to our quiet room to catch up with ourselves and review progress. We had a great venue, a very welcome grant, a fabulous and ever-expanding team of speakers and two outstanding musicians. Both were male, however, and we wanted to introduce a softer, lighter feminine element to the music. But we had no idea where to look. No sooner had the thought gone out than a few days later I happened to be speaking to a friend who ran a local holistic magazine in which we were planning to place a series of advertisements for the conference.

"How's it going?" she asked.

"Great," I answered. "But we're looking for a female singer to add to our team. Do you happen to know of anyone?"

"Actually, I do," she said. "A friend of mine, a sweet and gentle young lady with an amazing voice, is back on the scene and looking for work. I think she might be interested." As it turned out, Kym Chandler was ideal. Blonde hair and blue eyes with a voice like an angel, she was the perfect complement to Jami and Mark. Our team was complete.

All we needed now was for people to turn up!

We had set ourselves a bold and ambitious target of attracting one hundred people. Bearing in mind we had a small study group and a handful of interested friends, we were virtually starting from scratch after all. We designed and printed thousands of colourful, punchy flyers that we disseminated far and wide and planned a diverse advertising and marketing campaign to get our message across. But we soon realised that we needed something to hang our hat on, a catchy caption or unique concept to convey what the conference was all about. And then came *The Secret*.

Divine synchronicity or what? Originally published in 2006, the phenomenon that was *The Secret* had reached heady heights by 2007 and now everyone was talking about the law of attraction as though it had only just been invented! This book succeeded in popularising and bringing into the public consciousness one of the absolutely key spiritual principles. Suddenly we had found our advertising slogan: 'If you like *The Secret*, you will love this! The first UK New Thought conference for Abundant Living'.

It worked. People got the message and the bookings began to flow in. It was then that we employed a familiar strategy we called 'the snowball effect'. Linda and I were in fact no newcomers to event planning because, years before, we had created a social group called Essence to put on events with a difference, to have fun and to raise money for charity. Our inaugural event had been at the Community Centre in Hampstead, in the heart of the north-west London trendy suburb. Our plan was to provide food, drink and a disco at a nominal price and attract as many people as possible. The strategy was simple: set a date, produce an informative flyer and tell everyone we knew to tell everyone they knew. In a matter of a few weeks the news had snowballed, everyone was talking about this amazing party to be held in Hampstead, and people we didn't know were 'phoning us up to tell us about our own event.

On the night we were sold out, packed to the rafters. Following the success of this inaugural event, we planned a series of equally interesting activities with a difference, raised hundreds of pounds for a major London children's charity and gained valuable experience for the future.

That now served us well as we deployed the snowball effect again to promote an event that really was different. Bookings trickled in, frustratingly slowly at first, so we treated for a vibrantly successful conference and an increasing flow of bookings. What does this mean? We visualised clusters of envelopes coming through our letter box, containing dozens of booking forms and cheques, flurries of emails and enquiries and a positive, enthusiastic response to our advertising and circulars. Gradually the trickle became a stream and by the middle of March we had fifty confirmed bookings. Half-way there.

By the end of April the numbers had doubled and we had reached our initial target. But it didn't stop there, it didn't even slow down. One month before the conference we had achieved the staggering total of a hundred and fifty paid up registrations and the bookings were continuing to flow in from far and wide, from people we had never heard of, from all over Great Britain and Europe. A friend from Holland organised a party of around forty people. There were groups from Ireland, from Belgium, Portugal, Germany, Greece, Spain and Switzerland. There were a handful of people from the USA who happened to be visiting at the time and a determined couple from the Ukraine, who fought to get their visas in time. There were contingents from all over the UK, from Land's End to John O' Groats.

We had stumbled upon – been inspired to – a successful formula. The timing was perfect, allied to the wave of interest in *The Secret*, and the price was right. Everything was coming together, as they say in Science of Mind, 'in Divine Right Order'.

From nowhere, it was becoming a truly international event and by the end of June we had reached over two hundred advance bookings; and on the day of the conference a further thirty people turned up at the door for last-minute tickets. With the numbers now exceeding our wildest expectations, we set about the pleasant if rather time-consuming task of revising and upgrading our logistical planning. There was an increased need for more food, drink, refreshments and helpers, let alone the additional paperwork and planning. Our days, nights and weekends were fully engaged ensuring that the facilities were adequate to cater for well over two hundred people, and we enjoyed every minute of it.

By chance we had happened to hear of an excellent local caterer who lived just a few minutes away. At our initial meeting we had optimistically set a target of one hundred people but now we were having constantly to revise and upgrade our estimates. By the weekend of the conference, the caterers had to bring in extra staff and supply additional provisions to feed the hungry hundreds of guests and speakers. Somehow, like manna from Heaven, the food flowed in abundance and everyone was treated to an exceptional menu that would have graced a four-star restaurant. There were exotic salads and savouries for lunch and, on the Saturday evening, a sumptuous fish and vegetarian buffet. This in-house, local catering proved invaluable as it helped to keep the conference flowing and added to the community atmosphere.

For the visitors coming from abroad and from far-flung parts of the UK, it was necessary to arrange suitable local accommodation. Our guest speakers were to be lodged in a nearby Holiday Inn overlooking a marina, a picturesque setting particularly at night with the lights from the moored boats and barges creating a warm and inviting glow. We reserved a number of rooms at a local Premier Inn for our numerous overseas guests. We arranged a minibus to shuttle guests to and from the conference venue, and a team of willing volunteers to act as chauffeurs for the speakers. It was a meticulous, military-style operation but thankfully, on the day, everything worked perfectly to plan.

Dan, the helpful Steiner Events Manager, was an aspiring musician himself and offered to supply us with a very useful PA system. He was duly gratified when we invited him to sing a song or two before the main conference began. A friend from Southampton set up a superb sound system for us and did a brilliant job of recording and packaging the main conference talks.

Now there were tickets and programmes to design and print, flowers to order and extra volunteers to delegate various tasks to, from registration and ushering to helping out on refreshments and chauffeuring speakers. We were truly grateful to all the volunteers who made such a big difference.

The stage was set – though there was something missing there. With such a large platform area we needed additional colour to create an attractive, eye-catching focal point. Linda located swathes of brilliant purple velvet cloth that was ideal for draping over trestle tables, with banks of purple and silver helium balloons proudly pronouncing ABUNDANT LIVING 2007. Yet we still needed a colourful backcloth announcing the theme and title of the conference. It so happened that a young student teacher working in the Art Department of the Steiner School heard of this and offered to hand-paint a giant banner. Amazingly, in a few short weeks she produced a stunning piece of work that fitted the bill perfectly and provided the final piece of the jigsaw.

As the days ticked by there was a host of things yet to do and the walls in our study at home were covered with charts and schedules and last-minute memos and reminders. Then it was countdown to the big day.

It was carnival time in the village and a rare interlude of sunshine amidst a grey and drizzly few weeks. Linda and I had taken the afternoon off and were sitting in our back garden enjoying the sun while discussing final preparations for the conference. I had popped inside to make a cup of herbal tea when Linda rushed in, flushed with excitement.

"I've got a great idea!" she exclaimed, brimming with enthusiasm. "Let's create a conference theme song."

She had already scribbled down a page of possible lyrics so we put our heads together, bouncing ideas off one another, and before long came up with a catchy title, *Come Together*. It was a simple idea that resonated with the theme of the conference, people coming together to celebrate life, love and spirit. Within half an hour we had completed the song and all we needed now was to put it to music.

"Let's call Mark," we said together. Great minds think alike.

We made a `phone call to our UK-based musician, Mark Hughes. He was a maestro at putting words to music, but this was asking a lot of him. There were only a few weeks to go before the conference and he was busy with his own work whilst we were due away in a couple of days.

"Send me the lyrics," he offered, "and I'll see what I can do."

The last few months had begun to catch up with us. We were feeling tired and needed a break before the conference. Everything was in place, we had a handy assistant to look after messages, emails and last minute enquiries, so we planned a few days away in Cyprus to get some real sunshine. It's amazing what a week away can do. We arrived home refreshed and recharged, eager to hear what Mark had done with our song.

"Listen to this." Mark strummed his guitar and sang the lyrics over the `phone. It was terrific, instantly appealing and we loved it. He had cleverly welded the words and music into a simple yet memorable tune that perfectly fitted the mood of the forthcoming conference. In addition, he had designed a colourful sleeve and would be able to press dozens of CDs ready to sell. It was a proud moment when we received the final recorded version and played it on our hi-fi – and an even prouder one when Mark premiered the live performance at the conference.

Come together and celebrate.
Life is good and we are great.
Come together and let's create
a celebration of life.

Come together with spirits high.
Let's reach up and touch the sky.
Come together, you and I,
we'll come together for life.

Come together for humankind.
Come together and you will find
a celebration of life.
Come together.

Refrain

Hold hands (come together).
Link arms (come together).
Join minds (come together).
Come together for life, come together.

Words and music by Linda & David Serlin & Mark Hughes

Making History

After all the months of planning, the day finally arrived. It was a cool, overcast Saturday morning with a hint of rain in the air as we left home early for the Steiner Theatre to finalise arrangements and attend to a host of last minute preparations. To our surprise there was already a queue of at least thirty to forty people waiting patiently outside. Doors were not due to open until 9 a.m. but everyone was laughing and joking and seemed oblivious to the weather.

The next half an hour or so was a flurry of activity as we pre-pared piles of programmes, name tags and badges, before opening the doors to let in the eager early-comers. The narrow entrance lobby was soon packed with people keen to get into the theatre; and despite the inevitable queues everyone was in good spirits, happy to participate in such a historic event. A number of people had arrived on the off-chance of buying tickets at the door and our carefully organised team of helpers were almost overwhelmed by the sudden deluge of humanity as everyone converged in the entrance at the same time.

Then, like a slow motion movie, the day unfolded, taking on a life and momentum all of its own. Speakers and musicians arrived on cue. PA systems and microphones were checked, last minute food supplies were hurried in, a few tuning notes on guitars and the background buzz of animated chatter filled the air as people took to their seats and introduced themselves to their neighbours. Finally, it was time to begin.

With a surge of excitement, the adrenalin coursing through our blood, Linda and I sprang proudly onto the platform with microphones in hand to open proceedings. There was already such an incredible atmosphere we could hardly contain ourselves.

"Hello, Holland!" Dozens of hands sprang up.

"Welcome, Ireland and Scotland! Hello, all our friends from Europe." It was like the United Nations with vociferous contingents from Germany, Greece, Switzerland, Spain, Belgium, Portugal, Ukraine and America, with a very substantial home-grown support from all parts of the United Kingdom. We took it in turns to introduce our speakers and musicians and as the excited babble from our very lively audience began to subside the curtains were pulled back to mark the beginning of the first UK New Thought Conference for Abundant Living.

It was in fact the first ever Science of Mind Conference in the UK and, as we later discovered, the first New Thought Conference in the UK for nearly a century. We were indeed making history.

Standing together on the stage, looking out onto the massed rows of smiling faces stretching to the back of the auditorium, was an amazing feeling, hard to put into words. There was a welling up of emotions, a feeling of tremendous pride, joy and satisfaction, and an immense sense of achievement. It was one of those special moments that will live on, deeply etched and cherished in the memory.

We savoured every moment even though we had our hands full with supervising, organising, keeping an eye on everything and everyone, monitoring the programme, watching the clock... and still trying to be part of the event, to enjoy the talks, appreciate the music and bathe in the amazing, unique energy and atmosphere that was already beginning to build.

"Something's calling me…"

At 9.45 a.m. the rich, honeyed tone of Jami Lula's voice and crisp guitar sound rang out through the auditorium. The chattering soon ceased as hundreds of people turned their attention to the stage and the group of musicians assembled there.

"Something's calling me, a little bit deeper than I've ever been before."

Something had called us to create this remarkable gathering in the first place and we wondered what had inspired and enticed all these people from such diverse places and backgrounds to come and share the weekend with us. We had devised a very full programme, making use of every available minute. Dozens of talks, workshops and interactive sessions would be interspersed with and complemented by carefully chosen musical interludes. We wanted to make it a memorable, life-changing event that would have a profound and lasting impact on those who attended and make a real difference in people's lives.

Our charismatic keynote speaker, Dr Mark Vierra, took to the stage, striking an impressive figure highlighted against the purple and white backcloth and greeting the audience with a big, wide open smile.

"You know I love the UK, the people and the culture. You Brits could really teach us a thing or two," he quipped. His theme was New Thought, New Beginnings and his message was, "You have come here to do extraordinary things, to enjoy a greater, more abundant expression of life."

Mark was the perfect opener and his energy, enthusiasm and sense of humour had the audience hanging on his every word. His Californian charm, down-to-earth personality and tell-it-as-it-is wisdom was instantly appealing and challenged us to step out of our comfort zone and embrace a whole new realm of experience.

"What is it you think you came here for?" He was being more existential than circumstantial. A few people shuffled uncomfortably in their seats, wondering where this was all leading. He continued, reassuringly, "Nobody ever said that the reason you are here is to struggle. You came here to do extraordinary things. You came here to have, be or do whatever you can create and become in your consciousness. What you are grateful for expands. What you take for granted diminishes. Abundance is what the universe is all about. There are no plaudits for poverty. God's will is not for us to lead dowdy, miserable lives, but for greater love, peace and abundance, anything that does no harm to anyone else but that supports an expression of greater life. I like to think of God as Spirit, the infinite Creator or, as they say in *Star Wars*, The Force."

Mark paused for a moment as though contemplating a deeper thought. We realised that this was going to be an extraordinary weekend, an opportunity to break through barriers and challenge longstanding beliefs. Already we could sense a deepening of the atmosphere, a shift in consciousness.

"The study of Science of Mind," he continued, "is a preparation for mystical consciousness. There are many paths up the mountain [*a metaphor for spiritual growth*]. At the bottom of the mountain, all the religions have their own dogmas and doctrines, rituals and outer practices. But as you get higher up the mountain [*deepen your spiritual consciousness*] the teachings converge and seem to say the same thing: the One. We don't really want to get stuck at the bottom of the mountain."

Ernest Holmes, the founder of Science of Mind, was very practical in what he taught because he understood mystical teachings. He knew that if he could get people really to understand and apply the principles, they could get out of struggle and move up the mountain, grow in consciousness. It's all about having a more abundant life, more abundant health, finances, wellbeing and joy.

"There is a big difference," Mark reminded us, "in knowing the principles and putting them into practice. In Science of Mind we have a saying, 'Treat and move your feet.' We may all know intellectually what may be good for us, but actually doing it is another matter."

After this introductory talk, Mark invited members of the audience to share their experiences – called demonstrations – of the principles in action. While many people were new to metaphysical ideas, some here were already seasoned students of Science of Mind and a flurry of hands followed as several people volunteered. First to the microphone was a young man from Germany eager to speak, in near perfect English.

"I would like to share my story with you. I received a flyer about the conference and I knew I just had to be there but I didn't have the funds for the trip. I said to myself, 'Forget it, you cannot go.' Anyway, a couple of days later I was sitting in my office looking out the window when I had a strong feeling that somehow I just had to get to the conference, but I still did not know how. It had been a difficult day and I really needed something special to happen.

"Suddenly the `phone rang. It was a client from the UK I had been trying to contact for nearly a year. Up to now he had never returned any of my calls. Anyway, he apologised and asked what I wanted. I explained that I had a product that might be of interest for him. He said, 'Why don't you come to the UK and visit me?' So, I thought to myself, 'This is interesting, it seems like a demonstration going on here.' I got in touch with several other potential customers in the UK and organised some meetings, and this meant I did not have to pay for my flight – the company would pay for it! Then I heard from David that there was someone else coming from Germany and perhaps we could share a room to save costs. We got in touch and, though we had never met or spoken before, I discovered that not only did he live just down the road from me in Berlin but he was also a keen student of Science of Mind. Now that is what I call a demonstration!"

"My life had become chaotic," said an American lady who was living in London. "My flat was full of clutter and though I had been chipping away at it bit by bit there was still a huge pile of mail I had not opened for a long time. I paid my bills by direct debit so there was nothing like that to be concerned about. The other day I was looking for something in the pile when I came across an envelope I didn't recognise. Something pulled me to pick this one out and open it. It was the invitation to this conference.

"Thank God I found that envelope because I had been looking for some way to connect with the Science of Mind community in the UK and I had never met anyone who even knew what I meant. It felt like a miracle. Something energetically had made me pull out that particular envelope and open it, even though all the other mail remained unopened."

A radio presenter from Ireland, who hosted a popular show for personal growth and psychic development, was also keen to share his story.

"The station I work for specialises in country music and psychic development. It is an interesting mix. Anyway, one day a lady called in and explained that she worked as a nurse but her real passion was for singing country music. She wanted a career change but she didn't know where to begin or what to do. She worked long hours and didn't have enough time for singing. I suggested she send me a demo tape and she did.

"As it turned out, her CD was absolutely fantastic. She was really talented and so I broke all the rules and agreed to play her CD on air. The response was brilliant. Many of my listeners called in to say how good it was. Well, we had played her music, broadcast her songs and given her a moment of fame, which was great, but it didn't end there. That same evening one of the biggest television networks in Ireland called in to say they were looking for new talent for a forthcoming country music competition. They had discovered our radio station and tuned in to my show, and when they heard that CD they had thought, 'This is it.' Anyway, she went on the show and she won it!"

"It's extraordinary," Mark responded, "what can happen when you are open and receptive."

The secret is to remember that your current thoughts
are constantly creating your future. Visualise what you want.
Be grateful and act as if you have already received it,
take inspired action and leave the rest
to God, to Spirit and the universe.

The morning session had been overflowing with food for thought and now it was time for thought of food. A sumptuous buffet lunch awaited us as we filed our way out of the theatre into the nearby dining room. As the minutes ticked by, the spiralling queue for lunch seemed to be getting longer and longer, but nobody seemed to mind. In fact, people were taking the opportunity to stand and chat and get to know their neighbours. Lunch was no frugal affair. There was a lavish and abundant menu of fresh salads and hot savouries, all rounded off by homemade carrot cake and fruit salad.

Suitably nourished and recharged, we returned to the theatre at two o'clock for an appetising menu of afternoon talks and workshops. The weekend so far had been an absolute joy. Even the sun promised to break through the lingering clouds and interrupt the unseasonally cool weather, yet the energy and atmosphere inside the conference was so electric and energised that we barely noticed what was going on in the outside world.

Discover Your Hidden Healing Power was promised by one of the afternoon workshops.

How To Make Your Relationships Work the Spiritual Way was offered by New Thought minister Heather Andrews Dobbs.

Best-selling author Diane Harmony presented Five Gifts for an Abundant Life, while Dr Tom Sannar, an acknowledged expert on the life of Ernest Homes, explored The Mystical Secrets of Permanent Prosperity.

All the while, Linda and I were patrolling the corridors, popping in to catch a glimpse and snapshot of each talk and workshop, chatting, checking and catching snippets of wisdom here and there. With such diverse options people were spoilt for choice, but it had always been our intention to offer a rich and varied menu and leave no stone unturned in presenting the cream of New Thought and Science of Mind to the UK. The afternoon just flew by and the atmosphere was buzzing when we gathered back in the main theatre at five o'clock to the sound of Jami Lula singing, "Imagine there's no Heaven, it's easy if you try..."

In some respects, this already seemed like Heaven. A whole weekend of fabulous speakers, inspiring talks and music, fabulous food and hundreds of fun, joyful, like-minded people from all over the world. Does it get any better than this?

Mark took to the stage to round off the day session with a few final thoughts about *The Secret*. Indeed, it really was no secret anymore but there were still some misunderstandings and misconceptions that needed to be explained.

The law of attraction states that we tend to draw into our experience those things and situations that we focus on in our thoughts. But it's more than that. It's all about what's in our consciousness, the sum total of our thoughts, beliefs, attitude actions and feelings, which tends energetically to attract more of the same.

What we believe to be true about ourselves and our lives
tends to become our experience.
The outer world of form and substance
is but a reflection of our inner consciousness.

"Imagine yourself as a giant magnet," Mark explained. "You draw to yourself those things that resonate with the way you think. If you think a thought without a contradictory thought, then that thought goes out into the universal mind and returns to you as your experience. You are attracting like thoughts all the time. As within, so without. We each have our own frequency and vibration. We are like a human transmission tower. What we are thinking right now is going to create our future life, because thoughts become things.

"Let us consider – is what we are thinking right now going to create the future we want? I am not going to tell you how or what to think. It's your choice. But just having this awareness, that our thought is creative, that we are constantly attracting into our lives, gives us the opportunity to ask the questions, 'Is this what I really want to manifest in my life? Is what I am thinking right now going to take me in the direction I want? If what I am thinking right now were to manifest, would that be for my good?'

"All that we are now is a result of what we have thought. Our thoughts are creative and the creative process is about asking, believing and receiving. First and foremost we have to be clear in our own minds about what we want. Whether we are looking for harmonious relationships, peace of mind, health and well-being or something external, outside of ourselves. Success and fulfilment come in a variety of guises and are unique and subjective to each one of us. So, we have to be clear what we are asking for.

"Then comes the believing. This is where we need to 'act as if' – in thinking, speaking and believing that what we want is already so. If we are asking and affirming for a healing, we have to ask ourselves, 'How would it feel if the healing had already happened?' Of course, we would feel great. We'd be happy, we'd feel fantastic. So the secret is to feel it now. Then the receiving is easy. If we can feel as if it is already so, through the law of attraction the universe can support us. And the more we hang out in that feeling, the quicker the result. In Universal Mind, in Spirit, there is no time. There is only now and now is the perfect time.

"It's also important to feel good about ourselves," Mark continued, shifting the emphasis back to us. "Sometimes people get stuck in feeling bad about themselves. In the Bible we read about 'walking through the valley of the shadow'. There are those people who don't just pass through it, they pitch their tent there. The good news however is that love is the highest frequency, the highest possible vibration of thought. We know that love heals. We know that it feels good to receive love. It feels pretty good to give love too.

"A lot of people tend to expect the worst. They expect things to fail, fall apart and go wrong. That's using the power of expectation in the wrong way. We want to expect good things, success, health and abundance. In Science of Mind we have a saying, 'Expect the best and make it happen.' It's all down to attitude, and gratitude is a great attitude and will bring you more of what you want.

"You don't always need a reason to be grateful. Just being grateful gives you more reasons to be grateful. Thanksgiving before you have received is the highest form of prayer. Giving thanks in advance before you see any objective signs or demonstration is very powerful. In *The Secret* we are advised to visualise our good, but the piece that people miss is that they tend to visualise way into the future. The key is to visualise as if it is happening right now. What we focus on, we increase. If we focus on health, we increase health in our life. If we focus in wealth, we attract more of it. But if we focus on lack and limitation, we only bring more of the same into our lives."

You don't always need a reason to be grateful.
Just being grateful gives you more reasons to be grateful.
Thanksgiving before you have received
is the highest form of prayer.

"The secret is to be happy now. Be happy now because this is the life you've been waiting for. Don't wait 'til next week, next month or next year to be happy. When you are happy now, when you just choose to be happy, the universe looks back at you and says, 'Now there's a satisfied customer.' And what do we do with a satisfied customer? We give them even more to be satisfied with. You can choose to be happy, irrespective of outside conditions.

"There may still be things that aren't as you might wish them to be. But it will be easier to deal with them if you make a choice to be happy now. With happy, inspiring, uplifting energy it's easier to do good work in the world, because people like to be around happy people. A generation filled with hate will never bring peace to the world. We have to be at peace, with a generous, peaceful mindset, if we want to create a peaceful world. We cannot help ourselves or the world by focusing on the negatives. We can choose to be part of the problem or part of the solution. We can all focus on what's wrong with our lives, but let's focus on what's right and by the focus of our thoughts attract more of the same."

Mark went on to explore another intriguing aspect of the so-called law of attraction.

"We are constantly attracting into our lives. After years of habitually thinking in a particular way, we become fertile soil for certain types of experiences to manifest. In some respects, we almost welcome them. We magnetise and draw people and circumstances to us that harmonise with our habitual thinking – and sometimes we may be affected by other people's thoughts, intentions and desires. It is a complex issue.

"The law of attraction is a powerful force in our lives and the most important question we may ask ourselves is, 'What do I want to attract into my life now?' Our destiny is not cast in stone. If we are not happy with any aspect of our lives, if we don't like what's going on, we have the power to change, to change the focus of our attention to qualities like love, peace, health, healing and abundance. It is important to be for something and against nothing. So, let us ask ourselves, 'What are we for?'

"I am for peace. I am for joy. I am for bringing people together to love and appreciate each other. I am for gatherings like this. I am for having a good time!"

*We magnetise and draw people and circumstances to us
that harmonise with our habitual thinking,
and sometimes we may be affected
by other people's thoughts, intentions and desires.
The law of attraction is a powerful force in our lives
and the most important question we may ask ourselves is,
'What do I want to attract into my life now?'*

It had been a fabulous and fulfilling first day. Everything had gone to plan and even the minor hitches had given birth to some interesting new opportunities. At six o'clock the aroma of freshly cooked delicacies wafted through the corridors and a queue quickly formed, snaking its way towards the dining room. Many new connections had already been forged and animated conversation around the dinner tables suggested these would not be short-lived. This was time to refuel and recharge before a busy evening programme, due to begin at 7.30 p.m.

To cater for a number of people who had been unable to commit to the full conference, we had devised a special evening programme – a short event within the main event – to give people a flavour of what it was all about. On offer was an attractive package that included a three course meal followed by VIP seats for the evening session. This was a themed event of music and inspirational talks entitled A Celebration of Life, Love and Spirit.

The mantle of headlining the evening programme fell to Mark Antony Lord with music by Jami Lula and Mark Hughes. Mark Antony had arrived at the hotel the day before after a long-haul flight from Chicago, looking jet-lagged and dishevelled. Picking up on our obvious concern however, he had quickly reassured us, "Don't worry, I clean up well."

He kept to his word. We hardly recognised the dapper, clean shaven and well-groomed figure who bounded onto the stage immaculately attired in a smart white suit.

The early evening sunshine pierced the window blinds, sending ribbons of light across the crowded room. We had lost all sense of time and space, bathed in a unique and lofty atmosphere of spiritual communion. This newly fledged two hundred strong community shared a bond of friendship and interconnection that promised a lengthy shelf life. It was no transient, superficial experience; on offer was a life-changing opportunity for personal growth and transformation.

"Are you getting it?" With an explosion of raw energy, Mark Antony was in the zone, firing on all cylinders, inviting us to "Get metaphysical!" With his background in drama and dance, he had all the moves and forty-five minutes to win us over. He hit the ground running!

For a moment there was a stunned silence, a holding back from a slightly shell-shocked audience, who were not quite used to this brand of open-hearted, full-frontal spirituality. We held our breath wondering how Mark Antony's effusive, exuberant style of presentation would go down with a European audience. But our fears proved unfounded. Within a few minutes, as he recounted the story of his own journey of personal challenges, trials and tribulations – and how he had discovered his spiritual identity within a narrow-minded community – the audience quickly warmed to him. In fact, by the end of the weekend he had become one of the most popular of all the speakers.

"Here's the deal," Mark teased. "I am here to be fabulous! I am a divine creation. I am going all the way and I want to take you with me." Laughter and cheers of approval from a now fully attentive audience.

"You are here to answer a call," he continued, "to respond to an invitation, to go deep within yourself and awaken to your authentic power. You are here to be the best, the most fabulous self you can be. You are here to revel in the power and the presence of God, of abundance, of wisdom, of all that you need or desire." Little by little we were becoming captivated by Mark's infectious energy, enthusiasm and disarming honesty.

"When you walk in authenticity, when you live and move in this vibration, you are in the flow of well-being. Abundance is all around you. You become a living, moving law of attraction drawing to yourself good and greater good. You become a messenger for love. When you simply say 'Yes' to awakening your greatness and goodness, you become a messenger of love that says to everyone, 'Anything is possible.'"

By now we were so immersed in the energy and vibration of the experience, we truly believed that anything is possible. In that mindset, we were primed and ready to hear more about magic and miracles. When we are at home in the world of reality it may not seem so simple. But here was an opportunity to go deeper, to raise our consciousness and embrace a spiritual strategy that could transform our everyday lives. Mark was a master story-teller and cleverly intertwined his message within a tale that kept us guessing.

"A group of Buddhist monks," he began, "were charged with the task of moving a massive five ton, twelve-foot clay statue of the Buddha. It was a difficult and challenging task that stretched them to the limit. Many times along the way they asked themselves, 'Why are we doing this? What's the point? Let's give up and go home.'

"Late one evening when they were absolutely exhausted, they started to get clumsy and careless and dropped the statue in the mud. They were just about all in. They needed to rest and get some sleep. Then during the night one of the monks had a dream in which he saw the statue as being so valuable and precious that it woke him with a start. He daren't tell his fellow monks. They would no doubt laugh at him and think he was crazy. So he got up quietly and snuck out to where the statue lay on the ground, caked in mud.

"He had a flashlight with him and as he inspected the statue he noticed that when it had been dropped a crack had appeared. When he shone his light into the crack the light reflected back. He continued to chip away at the mud and clay that encased the statue and the more he chipped away the more the light shone back. He discovered that, underneath the mud and clay, the statue of the Buddha was pure gold.

"It turned out that several hundred years prior to this, a group of Siamese monks were being persecuted by the Burmese army and had concealed the golden statue in mud and clay so that the soldiers wouldn't find it. All the monks had then been killed so no-one knew the secret of what lay hidden inside the statue – that was, until now.

"Is this not true of our lives too?" Mark suggested. "But I think there was divine timing in the revelation of the golden statue, as many times along the way it could have been damaged, destroyed or even sold. Anything could have happened to it, but it was revealed at the perfect time. This is a story that relates to my life and possibly to your life too. We all have stories that cover and conceal the pure gold that lies within us. But today is the day we get to chisel away at the mud and the clay and awaken to the golden Buddha that is within each of us.

"I had a lot of clay, a lot of stories covering up the true light of my being. As a child, I knew that to reveal my true, authentic self could be dangerous. I was told, 'Who do you think you are?' I could have responded, 'I am a divine being of light! I am the love intelligence of the universe! I am it!' That's who we really are!"

There was appreciative applause and acknowledgment from the audience before Mark continued.

"As I look at my life, at the times and the stories that were most painful, I know they were there for a reason. I don't need to know what the reason was, but I do know there is a time for us all, when we can walk free from the mud and the clay, when we walk as our own golden Buddha. And that day can be now. But how do we chip away at the mud and clay? I tried everything, every type of therapy and remedy and they all helped a bit. But the most profound vibration we can use is the vibration of love. Love will wash away everything that is unlike itself."

After a brief break, Mark the master storyteller continued. We could have listened to him all night. He had the gift of keeping it simple, making it interesting and yet presenting an illuminating message that was real and relevant. Eyes and ears were glued to what he had to say next. It was as though he was talking individually and directly to each one of us. You could, as they say, hear a pin drop.

"We are each here by divine appointment. Each of us is here to be part of something so great that we cannot even begin to imagine. You know it's a vision because you cannot imagine how you can do it, and there's no evidence in the world to prove to you how it's going to happen.

"As you walk along this spiritual path, you may be called to be a teacher or a healer, to write a book or to create this gathering, to open a centre or to do something that from where you sit seems absolutely impossible. Then you will need to be careful with whom you share your vision – with the dolphins or the sharks. If you are swimming and get into trouble, the sharks will circle you and attack. But the dolphins will circle and protect you.

"When I am birthing a new idea, when I have some new inspiration, when I get really excited about an idea, I don't want to share it with the sharks. They will only tell me why I cannot do it, why it's impossible. You want to share these inspirations with the dolphins. This is the place where you can open up to what is burning inside of you.

"So, what is your vision? You are not going to find it in the world of form, because it is burning inside of you. Your work is to see the flame that consumes you like the burning bush. There may be signs in the physical world that point the way, but ultimately that vision, that big idea is planted in you and, as you water and feed it, it will grow. I wish for all of you the blessing I had of having a vision that first of all consumed me and then I watched it come into form effortlessly. It was wonderful. There was so much grace and ease and, the more I kept my hands off, the better it got.

"The Spiritual Center in Chicago of which I am the founder came to me in a vision. I saw everything. I saw where it was going to begin. I saw how it was going to form. I saw the whole thing from the beginning to the full expression of it. Not only did I see this vision, I felt it in my body. When I came out of meditation I felt, well, if Moses had this burning bush experience, that was what it felt like. I felt this vision with my whole body. I immediately knew this was what I was intended to do. Divine synchronicity gave me clear signs that I was on the right path.

"I was working in Chicago for a few days and one afternoon had to find somewhere to live. Walking in town I noticed a For Rent sign outside a building not far from my new Center. I knocked on the door and to my surprise the guy who opened it turned out to be someone I had known years ago. He happened to own the building and I got the apartment! I went back to California, collected my belongings, loaded my truck and drove halfway across the country to Chicago.

"The place where we began our services was the exact place I had envisioned in my meditation. It was the meeting room at the back of a big spiritual bookstore. The owner of the bookstore had been approached by several other churches, but ours was the only one he had said 'Yes' to. It was effortless, the whole thing, and what was really interesting was that when I went back to California and told people what I was doing they said, 'Wow, that's great. That's really courageous! You are so brave!' I heard that so much I started getting a little apprehensive as I wasn't feeling particularly brave. But my vision was so alive I didn't need courage. I didn't even think about it. I was being led by, fed by and moved by a vision that so consumed me that all I had to do was to show up every day.

"Before I opened my Center, I had twelve weeks of visioning meetings in the living room of my apartment. At the time I only knew a handful of people, my partner and one or two others. But people just started coming. Every Wednesday evening people just turned up. I cannot even remember how the word got out. I would look around the room at the twenty or thirty people gathered there and I wondered how on Earth did they get there? How could I have attracted this particular group of people? But I knew this was Spirit's doing. There was something at play greater than me, a vision that was calling me as well as all these people."

Listening to Mark Antony, it suddenly dawned on us that conceiving, organising and hosting this gathering, the first ever Science of Mind conference in the UK, had been our own burning bush experience.

Looking back, it had been a bold and courageous move, though at the time we had not given it a second thought – we'd had no doubt that Spirit was showing us the way.

Mark Antony's talk was followed by the angelic voice of Kym singing, 'How could anyone ever tell you that you're anything less than beautiful?' and then Dr Kathy Hearn concluded proceedings with a gentle prayer of thanksgiving. The lights dimmed shortly after ten o'clock on an amazing, heart-warming day.

A Greater Power

Sunday dawned with a vivid blue sky and a real feeling of summer in the air. Our musical maestro Jami Lula kicked off the day's proceedings with a vibrant version of *Something's Calling Me*. Looking refreshed and invigorated after a night off, our keynote speaker Dr Mark Vierra opened with a flourish.

The title of his talk was Treat Yourself to Success – Spiritual Mind Treatment Explained, a big subject but clearly Mark was up for it and on top form. Conference Day Two clearly had a new and different energy, as people had got to know one another and the speakers; we could focus fully on content now and dive deeper into spiritual wisdom.

Spiritual mind treatment, also known as affirmative prayer, is at the very heart of Science of Mind. It is the special factor that transmutes our spiritual hopes, dreams and aspirations into reality. Used with the right application, understanding and intention, it can create miracles in our lives. This is because it brings us within the orbit of true spiritual power, the very life force and intelligence that surrounds us and permeates every aspect of our being. Thus Spirit, or the Power for

Good, works through us and not to us. We are the channels through which miracles can happen.

"Ernest Holmes," Mark began explaining how it works, "developed a method of prayer based on spiritual principles and he called this method 'affirmative prayer', or 'spiritual mind treatment'. Holmes' method was based on principles that anybody could use and experience positive results. First and foremost, we need to know what we are praying for. We need to have purpose, direction and intention for our prayer.

"There are five steps in Holmes' method. In the first step we recognise and give our attention to a higher power, a Power for Good greater than we are – whether we call it God, Spirit, Infinite Intelligence or the Creative Mind. We then remind ourselves that this power is everywhere present, in all people and all things at all times. It is part of us, as much as we are part of it.

"In the next step, we identify that which we wish to manifest or realise in our lives and affirm that it is already so even though there may not yet be any outward signs or demonstration. In the fourth step we give thanks in anticipation of receiving our good, and in the fifth and final step we release our prayer into the universal law of mind, whilst letting go of any attachment to the outcome."

For many people, this might have been the first time they had ever encountered the concept of affirmative prayer, a form of prayer that does not involve beseeching or pleading with to a detached, distant deity. It is a process that takes commitment, application and perseverance and, above all, faith in that which is not yet apparent.

There is a higher Power for Good, greater than we are.
This power is present in all things at all times.
Affirm that what we desire is already manifest.
Give thanks in anticipation.
Release the prayer and let go of any attachment.

"You see, our words have power," Mark continued, "and the law of mind responds to them in kind. The words we speak become the law in our own universe. Sometimes we may say things to ourselves that are not kind and loving. Much of the messages that come at us from the media are not always good and positive. These are like seeds that are planted, which take root within us. That is why we need to mind our own minds, watch what we say to ourselves and what others say to us.

"There is our conscious thought that we are aware of and our subconscious thought that we are not aware of. Everything we have ever heard or been told resides in our subconscious. One day at school when I was just nine years old I had forgotten my homework. The teacher hauled me up in front of the whole class and shouted at me, saying what an awful child I was and that I would never amount to anything. So… look at me now! Though I have more or less recovered from that experience, it was imprinted in my memory. Occasionally in meditation or when I think back to the things that have had an effect on me, that teacher and that experience always shows up. The point is that what stayed in my subconscious mind was that I was not a good boy and that, apparently, I would never amount to anything. That stayed with me for a long time until I eventually reprogrammed that thought.

"Also, there is what we call the race consciousness, or what Jung called the herd mind, the thinking of the world that's coming at us all the time. If we don't take responsibility for what goes into our own consciousness and think for ourselves, then there is a world out there that will think for us. If we don't take responsibility for our own thoughts, then someone else will. If we allow the race consciousness, the collective mind, to impinge upon us, it may not be in the direction of our highest good.

"As we get out of bed in the morning, we have to affirm our life as we want it to be and not let the race consciousness determine who we are and what we can do. Every time we pray, affirm or meditate, we lift our own consciousness. We all need a daily spiritual practice that includes some form of affirmative prayer because, if we don't, we become subject to what everybody else is thinking and believing.

"I can be highly spiritual right up to when I leave my home," Mark smiled. "I pray, I meditate, I do my reading and affirmations. I have a whole spiritual practice in the morning before I leave my house. But sometimes I take the wrong turn and all that spiritual practice can just dissolve away as if I had never done it. So, this is the value of being in the world with other people, because other people can show us where we still need to be healed, where we have yet to love. I do my practice in the morning which is my anchor for the day. Then I go out and live my life. But often during the course of the day I may need to remind myself. When I am standing in line at the bank, it's good to have something simple and handy to refer to like the Science of Mind magazine or some affirmations – to make use of my time and do some spiritual work rather than judge, moan or complain and make my day and everybody else's a misery.

"In the Old Testament, the teaching was very much an eye for an eye and a tooth for a tooth, it was reward, revenge and retribution. In the evolution of consciousness on the planet, we had people like Buddha who talked about karma, the law of cause and effect, and Moses who came to bring the law. But as the consciousness of humanity continued to evolve there came Jesus who said, 'Yes, there is an eye for an eye and a tooth for a tooth, but there is also divine grace, forgiveness and the unique giving of Spirit.' The ancient covenant from the Old Testament was all about the law, but Jesus came to give the love.

"The new covenant is all about love and a practice that is so hard to master, forgiveness of self and others. In the old way, people were following the dos and don'ts. It was very much about how to behave, how to be good in the world. But as consciousness evolved, the new covenant changed all that. And it is through forgiveness that we may find true healing for ourselves and the planet."

The new covenant is love,
and through forgiveness we find true healing.

We had been treated to a metaphysical masterclass and the day had only just begun. The rest of the morning was devoted to a series of short workshops on subjects ranging from Ernest Holmes – the Man, the Mystic and the Message to Abundance – It's Not Just About the Money and Letting Go – the Power of Forgiveness. Our delegates were spoilt for choice but every workshop was well attended and could have gone on well past their deadlines.

At midday Jami and Kym gave a prayerful duet version of *Surely the Presence of God is in This Place*, creating an incredible atmosphere, a feeling of something very special happening.

"I don't know what you've been doing here," said Dan, the friendly Steiner Events Manager, "but it feels great!"

Dr Kathy rounded off the morning session with a few thoughts about the power of love. We need to move away from seeking love to being love, from victimhood towards empowerment, taking personal responsibility for our lives.

"If we don't do the healing work," she said, "instead of living out of love we live from reaction, with belief in limitation, fear and judgment. Next time you have a reaction to someone, ask yourself what is going on with you, what is being stimulated and triggered?

"I have a friend who says, 'I may have pushed your button, but I didn't install it!' This represents a moment of huge awakening without which we simply cannot move on to other levels of spiritual realisation. Ultimately, liberation comes when we cease to live from old ideas and false beliefs and live our lives from the greater truth of who and what we really are – spiritual beings having a human experience.

"What we teach in New Thought is that this is the truth of our being. We are created whole and complete and the qualities of the divine are the very essence of who we are. This is what we are here to express and when we are expressing the qualities of God, such as beauty, peace, love, gratitude and forgiveness, when we are functioning on these frequencies, that is when we are truly in tune with the infinite.

"It's always a matter of choice, whether we lead our lives out of reaction, from false beliefs of lack and limitation, or from the truth of who we really are, from wholeness, love, wisdom, beauty and joy. It's a moment-by-moment choice. We engage in life in such a way that our false beliefs can be easily stimulated. Rarely a day goes by when I may not experience some aspect of my life that needs to be healed, some part of me where I'm still waiting for the truth of wholeness to be revealed.

"As we grow and evolve spiritually, we move through various stages of consciousness. From giving up blame and being victim, to taking personal responsibility for what moves through our consciousness and for what we are creating in our life. We then move on to giving up control and surrendering to Spirit, ceasing trying to manipulate the law. We give up separation and realise we are the portals through which the divine Spirit is expressing itself. Ultimately, we actually become that which is expressing itself through us, the qualities of the divine. Across time and space, God's love expressed a divine idea and that idea was born as you and me. We accepted the assignment and came into form and here we are! And what a marvel it is that, out of all the shifts and changes in all of our lives, we have arrived here together.

"Think about this divine idea taking form as you. You were created in the image and likeness of a vast creative power, whole, perfect and complete. I invite you to connect with the highest truth of who you are and to think about your highest aspirations, your heart's desires, what Spirit would have you do to fulfil your purpose on Earth. Think of all the qualities of God – abundance, beauty, peace, wisdom and joy that you embody and say, I am that. And when someone says something wonderful to you, about you, say

'Thank you, yes, I am, yes, I know.'

"Dharma may be defined as our divine purpose, when all our gifts, talents, abilities and the truth of our being interconnect with what the world is calling for. Our collective assignment is to be the presence of God's love here on Earth. Whenever we are in a situation of conflict, bring forth peace. Every time we are in a moment of separation, bring forth love. Any time there is sorrow and we find the ability to offer the truth about joy, every time there is darkness and we bring light, then we are accessing and expressing God's love. The universal power of love has the ability to heal, to awaken and affirm the truth and bring forth the light. So, let's just get out there and do it."

In situations of conflict, bring peace.
In moments of separation, bring love.
Where there is sorrow, offer joy.
In times of darkness, bring light.

After lunch the summer sun, long overdue, made its welcome return and small groups of people meandered out to explore the grounds and gardens, deep in conversation and discussing dharma and divine purpose, deliberating over where we go from here. But before we had time to ponder further, the gong announced the beginning of the final, afternoon session.

It would be a packed workshop programme with Dr Tom Sannar inviting us to share The Five Secrets of Successful Living, Dr Kathy Hearn offering What's New about New Thought and Mark Antony Lord tempting us to participate in The Game of Life. We were making the most of this precious time as though joining in with the words of Jami Lula's song, *I won't waste one more minute of my life.*

By four o'clock we were back in the main theatre for a Q&A session, an opportunity to resolve any lingering questions with all the main speakers on the platform, hosted impeccably by Dr Roger Juline.

*'How would you describe metaphysics when speaking
to someone who was not even aware of this way of thinking?'*

"Metaphysics," explained Mark Antony, "is something beyond the physical. The spiritual truths inherent in this teaching are beyond that which we may see, read or even perceive. I believe that metaphysical principles can be applied to all religions, all sacred texts, to discover the deeper meaning.

"When I am speaking to someone from a more traditional or conservative background, I like to hear what their beliefs are, what beliefs are inherent in their teaching, and then to find some point of alignment."

*'The concept of God is associated with organised religion.
Is Science of Mind a religion or a philosophy?'*

"In Science of Mind," answered Dr Kathy, "rather than talk about religion we talk about spirituality, about a spiritual movement of awareness. People tend to shy away from the idea of organised religion and I say to them, 'Don't worry, because we are a disorganised religion.' There are many strings to it – the philosophy, the opinions, the teachings, the psychology – but ultimately it's all about New Thought."

*'A lot of people seem to think that The Secret is just about getting things.
But is there more? What is it really about?'*

"*The Secret*, the book and the movie, is all about the law of attraction, that our thinking brings about our experiences," Mark Antony offered. "We attract according to our thought. We also respond according to our thought. But the things we attract are really only symbols of what we really want, and it is our job as metaphysicians to see beyond the symbols without making any judgment.

"We are at the level of basement Math, while what we are talking about is advanced algebra. We may not understand the ins and outs, the complex, intricate details of how it all works, how spiritual law and principle governs the universe. What we do know is that it does work, and that there is a Power for Good, greater than us, that we can use."

As the Q&A session wound to a close, Linda and I had the sudden, sobering realisation that this fabulous weekend, this amazing conference gathering that had consumed so many months of planning and preparation, was coming to a close too. We could hardly believe how quickly the time had flown.

We had wanted to bring the essence of Asilomar to the UK, but in essence we had brought Asilomar to the UK: this was not just a taster, it was the real deal. We also realised in this moment that if we wanted to share such wonderful, positive, practical philosophy with others, rather than repeating what we had heard from someone else, then we would have to use it, study it and teach our own unique brand of New Thought.

"It's really very simple," said Dr Mark, closing the conference with a final few words of wisdom to sum up what had been an extraordinary weekend. "The truth is that God is all there is. When we talk about God, we are not referring to something external, outside of us. We are talking about the power and the presence, the love and the life, the divine intelligence that resides within each of us.

"Even when life may feel out of control, the one thing we always have control over is our thought, whether what we are thinking right now is helping or hindering the situation. As we grow and expand spiritually, a fundamental quality of a mature spiritual consciousness is to take responsibility for our lives. By taking responsibility for everything that happens to us, the good and the not so good, we assume the ability to choose how we respond to everything that happens to us.

"To a large extent, we are where we are because of past thinking and behaviour. If we want things to be different, to change, it's up to us to change our thinking and to remind ourselves that we can have and be whatever we become in consciousness." His words rang round the packed auditorium, bringing ancient wisdom up to date in terms we could understand.

"Every day we have a choice. We can choose to be happy, to be grateful, to count our blessings. We can choose to acknowledge the God within, the power and the presence that resides within us because ultimately there is only God. God is all there is."

This was endgame time, nearing the finale of a fabulous weekend and feeling that warm afterglow, like having had a satisfying meal and just wanting to sit back, relax and digest what has gone on. It had been only two days, but our world had changed for the better and nothing would be quite the same again. Dr Kathy stepped onto the platform to give the closing blessing.

"It's been so wonderful to spend this time with you. This truly has been an experience to remember, the ripples from which will continue long after the lights have dimmed and the last fond farewells have been made. On behalf of all of us who have come from all kinds of places, thank you so much for your warmth and friendship. This is the beginning of some wonderful connections that I know will last through time.

"So, let's go within, take a deep breath and feel the love and the joy of the past few days. Let's give thanks for the beautiful music, the wonderful talks, for every single moment of this experience we have had together. I know that the great loving intelligence within us knows just what to do with all that's been said, heard and felt, and that there is something taking place that will have transformed us forever. We are different people from having walked through this experience in each other's company. I know that because we have been together and shared together, that we carry a piece of each other wherever we are, that the love that is the truth between our souls supports our unfoldment as well as the unfoldment of New Thought and Science of Mind here in the UK.

"As we go out into the world to be whatever our Spirit would have us be, loving, free, powerful and abundant, the love and the joy we have experienced here may be expressed out into the universe. We give thanks for this realisation, accepting even greater good than we have yet known. We know it is done and with loving thanks we let it be, and together we say, 'And so it is.'"

The 2007 Conference for Abundant Living closed with hundreds of people standing together, holding hands and for the final time singing our conference theme song, *Come Together*. It was moving, a unique and special experience that would linger long in the memory.

Then one by one people filed slowly out of the theatre and into the late afternoon sunshine. For many, the weekend had been a revelation, an introduction to a whole new way of thinking. For some it had literally been life-changing. For Linda and me it had been the most exhilarating, rewarding, enlightening and fulfilling (if exhausting) experience that would shape our lives for years to come.

On that sunny Sunday afternoon, we could hardly have anticipated the ripples from that first conference that would inspire a whole new generation of Science of Mind events, workshops, seminars and gatherings from Bournemouth and Southampton to Geneva and Amsterdam.

That evening we arranged a farewell dinner for our speakers, musicians and VIP guests, at a vegetarian restaurant overlooking the nearby canal, the sounds of the barges and longboats tinkling at their moorings in the background while overhead a panoply of twinkling stars high in the night sky reflected the magic of the weekend. After a lively and entertaining evening, we walked back over an arched bridge to escort our guests to their hotels and waiting taxis. In just two or three days we had become like family and, as we bade our final farewells, we somehow sensed that this was not the end but just the beginning of something beautiful, of an extraordinary new chapter in our lives.

The next few days were spent tying up loose ends, dealing with finances, paying bills and a myriad of other business details. We were still on a high and enjoyed reading the dozens of emails, letters and texts that now came our way. Clearly, the event had made a deep and lasting impact on many people.

'Brilliant, a total celebration of life, love and spirit. It was wonderful to have so many souls on the same wavelength. I not only enjoyed myself, I received much needed guidance and confirmation that I should not doubt the universe.'

'What a wonderful weekend. I had a great time and it was so inspiring to meet so many openhearted people in one place. This has to be the beginning of something beautiful.'

'It was great to hang out with positive, like-minded, kind-natured people. Thank you so much for all your commitment and hard work in bringing people together from all across the globe to share and experience. I was honoured to be present.'

'The teaching was wonderful and inspiring. I loved the fellowship, beautiful togetherness and healing energy. The music was so uplifting, and I am so grateful to have met so many wonderful people. The spiritual connection was very profound.'

'I enjoyed my day at the conference. I came alone, but I did not feel alone at any time. I have been left with so much to think about.'

'A big thank you for such a wonderful, magical, inspiring, amazing, uplifting weekend! It shall live on in my heart for a long time. I have met some wonderful human beings and I feel more happy, inspired, peaceful, balanced and positive about things than ever before. Thank you again for having your vision and putting it into practice.'

And that's exactly what it was, having a vision and putting it into action. From the first moment, the idea had quickly taken shape, gained momentum and come to fruition. We had taken a giant leap of faith, said a big 'Yes' to Spirit's invitation and watched in awe as things had miraculously fallen into place (albeit with a lot of hard work and energy!).

We wondered what Spirit had in mind for us next.

The Miracle Is You

We were experiencing a conference hangover, an unusual condition caused by prolonged exposure to beautiful music, lovely people, inspiring talks and profound spiritual wisdom. It had all been a bit of a dream and we still hadn't fully come back down to earth. Everyday chores and routines seemed a trifle mundane compared to the thrill and excitement of the past few days, one of those peak experiences that stand out as a significant landmark along life's journey. Our event had brought a lot of people together and forged many deep and long-lasting connections. For Linda and me, it had certainly deepened our connection with Science of Mind, the philosophy and the teachings, which now sat very comfortably with us, reinforcing what we had always thought, felt and believed.

Within a week or so, though, with things slowly getting back to normal, we started to have itchy feet: we'd had such a great time that we wanted to keep the feeling going. So barely had the dust settled when Linda and I both came up with the same idea.

"Let's go to Asilomar!"

There were barely three weeks until the Asilomar Conference in the USA was due to begin and we would be lucky to get a place, let alone flights. The logistics seemed daunting. Frantic 'phone calls followed, flights were booked (amazingly Virgin happened to have three seats left), hotels were arranged and the final few places at Asilomar were secured. Somehow, with a little help from our friends, we had managed to get it all together in a few frenetic days and, barely a month after the end of our own landmark conference, we found ourselves heading to Heathrow Airport on our way to yet another spiritual adventure.

Gordon Higginson, our early spiritual teacher and mentor, had advocated going on a spiritual pilgrimage every now and again, to refresh the soul and reconnect with the Source, with one's spiritual home. Asilomar was our pilgrimage and as we walked up the wooden steps into Reception to be greeted by a chorus of 'Hey guys, good to see you again' it really did feel like coming home. There was a friendly familiarity that allowed us to ease effortlessly into the routine. Yet here there was always a pleasant surprise just around the corner.

The theme this year was One Human Family – the Power of Belonging. After an early dinner we set off to Merrill Hall, the hub of the community. There were nearly nine hundred people in the auditorium and the atmosphere was electric, our attention immediately grabbed by the artist sitting and singing at the piano.

"There is only love. Love that heals, love that sets you free, there is only love…"

We were mesmerised by the rich tone and resonance of the voice and by the haunting melody that was captivating the audience. A friendly neighbour told us that this was Michael Gott, an artist with something outstanding and impressive about the man, his music and his voice. My immediate thought was that if we ever organised another conference – and we hadn't had the slightest intention or desire to do so – we would have to get Michael Gott to do the music for us. It was an incongruous idea that struck us both like a bolt out of the blue,

116

but in this energy and excitement seemed totally realistic, only to be reinforced by what we were shortly to experience.

There was also something extra special about the vibrantly attractive, red-haired lady who took to the stage next. Karen Drucker was funny, entertaining, full of life and humour, and when she sang the beautifully emotive words to her song *The Face of God* she brought the audience to tears. We became instant fans. Karen would make a fabulous addition to our already expanding hypothetical musical team, making a superb partnership with Michael Gott. We were getting carried away with ourselves in this Mecca of creative thought where hopes may be realised and dreams can come true. Something within was stirring and seeds were being planted for the next stage of our spiritual journey.

Being at Asilomar served not only to recharge our spiritual batteries but also to fire our imagination and inspiration for future work. We enjoyed walks by the ocean, taking in the smell of the sea and the energy of the breeze that blew across the bay. The sporadic afternoon sunshine warmed our bodies whilst the music and talks nourished our hearts and minds.

One afternoon towards the end of the week, we thoroughly enjoyed a workshop by two gritty New York 'New Thoughters', Elizabeth and Michael Arrot Rott, authors of the best-selling book *Shortcut to a Miracle*. This was down-to-earth, no compromise, old school metaphysics by two highly respected New Thought teachers who worked as a team and impressed with their humour and veteran wisdom. We walked away with a signed copy of their book, which still serves us well, with its portentous inscription, 'Enjoy your miracle, your miracle is you!'

We had become accustomed to miracles, those serendipitous, unforeseen turns of events that confound reason and remind us that, with God, all things are possible. This way of thinking was a far cry from what we had been brought up to believe, that miracles happen, if at all, way out there, out of our control. Here we were being shown that we are the channels through which life may weave its wonders.

God can only do for us what God can do through us. That is some food for thought.

We are the channels through which
miracles can happen.

A trip to California would not be complete without a few days chilling out on the beach at Santa Monica. Suitably recharged and refreshed, we felt ready for the journey home and to resume normal life. Our focus was very much on developing our study group, putting the principles into practice and getting back into everyday activities after months of single-minded preoccupation with the conference.

In the background, however, was a nagging feeling of unfinished business, a restless and growing urge to do something more. We were increasingly feeling like the protagonists in a spiritual drama, waiting for our next assignment. And sure enough, over the coming months a clearer and more detailed vision began to emerge of what our next mission might be.

Thursdays had become our spiritual evenings. Linda and I had formed a pleasant routine of sitting together, tuning in to Spirit, listening to music, lighting a candle and saying a prayer, doing some affirmations or treatments, maybe some absent healing – and discussing ideas and plans for the future. At the back of our minds, still lingering like some long-lost friend, was the possibility of planning another UK conference. With the dawn of the New Year, the idea slowly began to take shape and we felt the urge and inspiration to do it all again. We had learned lessons and gained experience; now we wanted to put some new ideas to the test and take things up a notch with plenty of time to prepare.

At an Extraordinary General Meeting of our Executive Planning Committee (Linda and I), we quickly reached a consensus. Top of the agenda was setting a date and finding a venue. While we felt excited at the prospect and were prepared for a long haul, we could not have anticipated the all-encompassing, totally absorbing, incredibly time-consuming process that would engulf our lives. Still, we set a date for a weekend at the end of June, 2009, and Abundant Living Part Two was on track.

Finding a suitable venue was our first priority. This time we envisaged having everything under one roof, conference, accommodation and catering. Using three different locations had been fun before but a lot of time, energy and expense had been spent chauffeuring guests and speakers back and forth. We wanted a classy venue that would convey the character and theme of the conference and offer a comfortable and convenient environment for people to relax in and enjoy.

The hunt was on and many a weekend was spent exploring the countryside of Hertfordshire, visiting a variety of country hotels, halls and stately homes, but none were suitable. They were either too grand or too small, too expensive or just unavailable on the dates we required; indeed, many were booked for years ahead. So we did what all good metaphysicians would do: we treated, we affirmed and visualised the ideal location at an acceptable price. Then we let go.

One Monday morning, I was heading down the A41 for a meeting. The sun was shining and it was a glorious day full of promise. I had taken this route countless times and passed by the Watford Hilton Hotel without a second glance, but now something nudged me to stop and go inside. Perhaps it was the large banner advertising 'newly refurbished conference facilities'!

With a few minutes to spare, I stepped into the spacious, modern lobby and felt a sudden frisson of excitement. It looked good, felt smart and professional, and I could already visualise dozens of people arriving from all over the country wheeling in their luggage and meeting up with old friends. The Events Manager was busy at a meeting but would see me if I could wait a while, and in the meantime I was invited to look around the hotel. As I walked down the lushly carpeted steps into the hotel ballroom,

I knew instantly that this would be perfect, easily accommodating the numbers we anticipated. But would it be available at the right price?

The Events Manager was helpful but doubted whether the conference suite would be available for the weekend in question during peak season. I waited patiently in her office and held my breath while she made several 'phone calls and then left to consult with her colleagues. After a few minutes she returned with a big smile on her face, looking even more surprised than I was. Apparently, not only were the facilities available that weekend but, if we were able to confirm quickly, she could offer us a substantial discount.

I was a little taken aback by the speed of events, but swept away with the excitement of the miracle. There was a large meeting room adjoining the ballroom, ideal for workshops or breakout sessions, and the hotel could offer us a number of bedrooms for overnight guests at a special discounted rate. Add to that free parking, use of the leisure and spa facilities and reasonably priced in-house catering. I couldn't wait to tell Linda. She was impressed by my enthusiasm but wanted to see for herself so the following day we both returned to the hotel to have another look around.

"I don't like it," she exclaimed. "I love it!"

We agreed that we need look no further so without further ado we confirmed the dates, paid a deposit and began discussing the logistics for our forthcoming event. A priority was the discussion of menus and catering. After our experience of the lengthy queues at the first conference, we wanted to offer an abundant and varied menu, slickly served buffet lunches and a first class two-course evening meal on the Saturday. We wanted to offer an attractive, value for money all-inclusive package of superb food, exceptional music, outstanding talks and a conference experience second to none.

The next item on the agenda was to book a top-notch team of speakers. We had already agreed that if we were ever do another conference, we must get Dr Roger Teel as our keynote speaker. His talks were familiar to us, as was his relaxed style and dry sense of humour.

He was a man of great wisdom and experience and to have him as our main speaker would be a blessing and a terrific coup. Dr Roger was the Senior Minister and Spiritual Leader of the Mile Hi Center for Spiritual Living in Denver, Colorado, one of the largest New Thought centres in the world with a membership in the thousands and a regular Sunday service attendance in excess of fifteen hundred.

He was a much sought-after speaker who travelled widely, headed numerous organisations and was at the cutting edge of the New Thought movement. We were thinking big, going for the best (and, in this case, aiming Mile Hi). An email to his secretary explained the background to the conference and how much we would be honoured to welcome Dr Roger and his wife Erica to England. As anticipated, though, he was booked for years ahead... His secretary promised to check things out and get back to us as soon as possible.

Several days later her email arrived and we could hardly believe our eyes. "Dr Roger would be delighted to attend." Apparently, he had just one free week in his entire schedule, which happened to coincide with our conference weekend. With the definite commitment of such a popular and prestigious keynote speaker, we were now on course to expand our team of speakers and recruit some outstanding musical talent. Naturally, we remembered the two exceptional musicians we had seen at Asilomar, Michael Gott and Karen Drucker. Michael's relaxed, effortless style of music, embroidered by richly haunting melodies and soul-searching lyrics, had quickly won us over and he would make a fabulous partnership with the ebullient Karen. Getting one of these would be a coup, getting both would be a miracle.

We believed in miracles.

When Michael Gott received our invitation, he responded immediately and with typical enthusiasm.

"Count me in," he declared. "I'll be there."

Then Karen also responded with an emphatic 'Yes', saying that she loved England and the opportunity to visit the UK and play at our conference would be a dream come true for her too.

Inspired by these early successes, we sought to add extra gems to our team of speakers. David Leonard came with a sparkling recommendation from Karen Drucker, "You will just love him." David was Senior Minister at the Huntsville Alabama Center for Spiritual Living and was fun, dramatic, entertaining and very likeable. (Anyway, with a name like that we just had to book him, since my name is David and my father's Leonard.)

Dr Kathy Hearn, who had graced our first conference, joyfully accepted too, adding an extra touch of class and elegance as Community Spiritual Leader for Centers for Spiritual Living. With our British musician, Mark Hughes, also on board we already had a fabulous line-up. But we felt there might just be room for one more participant, someone a little different…

We had joined the International New Thought Alliance and had been receiving *New Thought*, their quarterly magazine, for some time.

One particular article now caught our attention, by an LA-based writer, metaphysical teacher, nutritionist and raw food expert, Dr Susan Smith Jones. She had an unusual angle on New Thought and we thought she might add a little bit of spice to proceedings. After a series of `phone calls and emails we eventually managed to locate her and discuss the possibility of coming to the UK. She had just published a book on raw food and was keen to gain a more international audience, so the prospect of speaking and doing a workshop or two at our conference instantly appealed to her. We arranged a dinner date to meet and talk things over.

The only thing was – the dinner was to be at the Budding Buddha macrobiotic restaurant in downtown Santa Monica, California!

Well, summer would not be the same without a trip to the States and a visit to Asilomar. We had already tied up the key logistics for the 2009 conference and we had the outlines for our advertising and marketing campaign. It was time to take a break and where better than a trip to Asilomar and a few days chilling out in our favourite beach resort of Santa Monica?

It didn't take us long to shake off the cobwebs and acclimatise to the warm Californian sun as we browsed through the chic shops and boutiques of Third St Promenade. We reserved a table at the restaurant and waited patiently for Dr Susan to arrive as we scoured the menu. She walked in sporting a big, broad Californian smile, relaxed and easy-going and 'interestingly different'.

The author of several best-selling books, she was passionate about raw food, healthy eating, New Thought and the prospect of coming to the UK. Over brown rice, tamari sauce and organic tofu, we learned that she enjoyed hiking in the mountains at dawn, watching the sunrise or sitting quietly meditating in the silence. We were impressed and immediately agreed that she would make an attractive addition to our team.

From Santa Monica we headed to Anaheim for our annual fix of Disneyland magic, then spent the last few days of our holiday relaxing by the pool back at our hotel. With soft music playing in the background, palm trees swaying in the breeze and the warm sun glinting off the water, it was an idyllic, dreamlike setting. We wondered how we might transport some of that Californian magic back home to the UK and turn our dream into reality.

The next few months flew by as we designed and printed eye-catching colour brochures and posters, planned an ambitious publicity campaign and compiled a mailing list. We wanted to make this conference even more professional, even better than the first. A terrific sound engineer, Matt, would handle our sound system and the recording of music and talks, whilst the hotel staff served our every need, providing first class menus. A whole posse of volunteers were recruited to help out on the day.

Change your Thinking – Change your Life would be the theme, a simple and clear message.

We planned meticulously but even we could not have arranged the heatwave that bathed the UK at the end of June. When our American guests arrived from across 'the pond' they could hardly believe it – it was like home from home. And tired and jetlagged though they were after long haul flights from Dallas, Denver, Atlanta and Los Angeles, there was an obvious mood of bonhomie and we could see how well they all gelled. These were professionals, used to working as a team. However, the best laid plans…

Unforeseeable glitches threatened to derail all our endeavours. Firstly, unbeknownst to us, a wedding party had been booked into the ballroom for the Friday night, meaning that we couldn't get access to set up for the opening. Yet it's amazing how a crisis can bring out the best in people. Matt volunteered to come in after midnight to set up the sound system and the hotel events team promised to have the ballroom set up immaculately by the morning. We had to trust them and let go of any concerns; after all, we were working for Spirit. A strange calmness then came over us.

Next morning, we held our breath as we opened the doors – everything looked fantastic, with purple and silver helium balloons cascading over the stage, which boasted a colourful backcloth proudly announcing The 2009 New Thought Conference for Abundant Living.

But then, just as we were welcoming guests at Reception, the shrill shriek of a fire alarm pierced the air, shattering the early morning peace and sending people scurrying all over the place! Guests began emerging from all over the hotel in varying states of undress, some with towels draped around them and others with faces bearing incomplete make-up or shaving cream. A bewildered throng gathered in the car park as a tannoy announcement apologised "for the inconvenience". Actually, people seemed remarkably congenial and used this opportunity to introduce themselves and chat to their fellow guests, breaking the ice and creating a sense of camaraderie that was to characterise the whole conference.

The source of the alarm was traced to the breakfast room and overzealous use of a double-barrelled toaster!

A Dance of Awakening

Whilst our first conference had been full of energy and exuberance, breaking new ground, we had grown spiritually and this time it was about revelation, healing and finding a higher vision. We were going deeper, providing the space, hopefully, for major shifts to take place.

The day opened with Karen Drucker singing, appropriately, *Thank you for this day, Spirit, thank you for this day*. Linda and I stepped onto the platform to introduce our keynote speaker, Dr Roger Teel, from Denver, Colorado, having rehearsed the procedure a hundred times. But at that moment, a wave of warm, loving energy embraced us; we abandoned our script and spoke from the heart, sensing an extraordinary and magical feeling of real connection. Relaxed and suntanned in a smart cream jacket and grey trousers, Roger certainly looked the part as he opened his talk with a startling observation.

"I am here to tell you that something new is happening in this life of ours. Old forms are crumbling and the new is giving birth. I want you to know that, if you want to be a part of this change, then you are in the right place.

"There are reasons that you are here that you may or may not be aware of, reasons that are not just about the people you will meet, the networking you will do or the friendships and connections you will make. There is a higher reason for you to be here, which may only be revealed as the weekend unfolds.

"Many of you are here because there is something within you urging you to go for it! There is a power in the universe that will celebrate when you take the leap, when you truly believe in yourself, when you no longer need any guarantees. Our greatness, I suggest, our power, is in our willingness to stretch our wings and fly no matter how things turn out. When we challenge ourselves to boldly leap and heed our spiritual purpose, then only good can come out of it. We will find that the old way is not the only way and that there is always something better. Sometimes the voice of Spirit, of divine intuition, may speak to us softly and quietly. Listen to it, be sensitive to it – and say 'Yes'."

We could really relate to what he was saying. We had ourselves taken a bold step, in fact a giant leap of faith, in creating these conferences in the first place. It had been a lot of hard work and we could have taken the easy path and let somebody else do it. But Dr Mark Vierra had reminded us on that portentous day at Asilomar not to wait for somebody else. "You are somebody!" he'd said.

"As we study the power of thought," Roger continued, "we realise that there are moments when something moves us, when we may have an inclination, an inspiration, a new idea which may need to be nurtured, guarded and protected from doubt, fear and limiting beliefs. When you feel these inclinations, cherish them, honour them and follow them, for they may open the door to a depth of richness within. The universe has many treasures to offer you. They may come through the words of the speakers this weekend, but they are really only echoes of the wisdom that already resides within you. If we take dominion over our thoughts, then we really begin to change our lives.

"Most of our habitual thinking is simply pulling from old sources, from times of reaction and belief in limitation. But there is a larger field, a universal mind that responds to our deeper feelings and thoughts and brings them into reality.

"There are times, however, when there may be a dissonance between our surface yearnings and our deeper conclusions about life. The subconscious mind does not think rationally. It is like a sponge. It accepts whatever we deeply believe and give our emotional energy to. If we have had a difficult or disappointing experience in life, we may soak it up and store it in our subconscious for it only to resurface and tell us why we may not enjoy a loving and fulfilling relationship. We may have grown up believing that relationships are just too painful, or we may have grown up believing, and were taught, that money was the root of all evil so we should keep away from it and not be tainted by it. If our deeply held beliefs are sabotaging what we desire most in our lives, then we need to transform our subjective conclusions, welcome new experiences and enter the state where miracles can happen. When there is nothing in our conscious or subconscious mind that may disagree with what we desire then, all of a sudden, our dreams may manifest.

"Our thoughts are creative. But we are not our thoughts. We are the ones who choose our thoughts – or choose to allow old thoughts to surface in our awareness. We are the observers of our thoughts. When a thought of lack or limitation comes up, we often tend to identify with it and give it form. We say, 'Yes, that is true.' Then we totally merge with it until it operates and expresses itself through us. Yet as we observe the content of our thoughts, we realise we have the power to do something different, to initiate a new thought. Quantum physics tells us that everything in the universe emerges out of a quantum field of intelligence and energy, that thought is primary and form follows. Whatever thought resides within us, at whatever level, has the potential to become form. We don't have to control every single thought or feel guilty that we thought them. But in the awareness of our thoughts we can – if we choose – just let them go.

"What we are doing here at this conference is attempting to reset our vibrational field, the field of awareness through which we may transform the deepest beliefs we may have about ourselves and become channels for more spiritual mindedness. Many of us still have some form of resistance going on, old beliefs that are getting in the way, sabotaging our good. If there is any area of our lives which is not working, this is what may be happening, whether we are conscious of it or not. This is what we are here to discover, whether we are saying 'No' at a deeper level and resisting our good.

"The first step, then, is to observe our thoughts, to be aware of our beliefs and conclusions about life and, from time to time, to think a new thought, reminding ourselves that we are co-creators with the universe. The second thing we must do is to have a clear idea of what we want. The universal substance takes shape according to the mould of our thoughts, which need to be clear and definite for the universal energy to flow into form.

"It doesn't serve us, therefore, to be caught up in complaining. To complain about what has happened in the past, about what has been, only creates a mould for more things to complain about, with a belief less in possibility and more in limitation.

"Let us be aware of how we want our life to be, what the deepest desire for our life is, recognising that whenever we create a new dream, resistance will emerge and all the reasons why not. But the universe works in mysterious ways. If we have a clear idea in mind that is not coming from the complaints or shoulds, or from what other people say we can or cannot do, but from something deep within, from that clear mould, then pure creation can take place. Remember, we have the power. We are the children of an abundant universe. We are pure creation waiting to bring us to our higher good. We are to have great lives, to be emissaries for a new awakening."

Our thoughts are creative but we are not our thoughts.
We are the ones who choose our thoughts
or choose to allow old thoughts to surface.
As we observe the content of our thoughts,
we realise we have the power to initiate a new thought.
When there is nothing in our conscious or subconscious mind
that may disagree with what we desire
then, all of a sudden, our dreams may manifest.

Great minds, billionaire industrialists, successful entrepreneurs, scientists, inventors and artists, and New Thought authors from the past like Wallace Wattles and Napoleon Hill, all knew, understood and used the principles of the law of attraction long before the phenomenon had entered the popular public domain. 'What we think about, we bring about', has become a commonly accepted interpretation of the principle, but there is far more to it.

"Everything is twice created," explained Roger, "first in mind as an idea, a spiritual prototype, and then clothed in form as the thing. The law of attraction doesn't actually bring anything to us, it brings things through us. We must work on ourselves to have our circuits open to allow ourselves to own the vision, to be congruent and in alignment with our dreams."

So 'Ask, believe and receive' is too simplistic. When we affirm, make a request or place a cosmic order, as they say, it is just the tip of the iceberg and a whole lot more has to happen before we may see an end product. What matters most is what we are thinking, doing, feeling and believing day by day. Our everyday consciousness – the sum total of our thoughts, beliefs, attitudes and actions – needs to be in alignment with what we wish to manifest.

Suppose we wish to change jobs, to move house or establish a new relationship: how would we actually feel if it came about, do we feel ready and worthy of this change or is our subconscious silently resisting? Sometimes we may be aiming high but with unrealistic expectations that exceed what we are comfortable with; whatever our aspirations, they have to sit comfortably with us or the subconscious will simply reject it.

"One of the most beautiful aspects of New Thought philosophy," Roger clarified, "is that it is designed to bring us into self-mastery in every area of our lives. There is no reason why we should not prosper, or be limited or lacking materially. We must ensure however, that we use the law of attraction in alignment with whatever is for the highest good and deeper sense of peace. The more we work with the law, we realise that it is not so much about getting but more about being. The law of attraction reflects back to us who we have become."

'We must become more
if we want to attract greater good into our lives.'

ERNEST HOLMES

"The real purpose of the law is to reflect our enhanced state of being. The business at hand is not to view it as some outside principle that may bring some greater good into our life, but to refine our own inner awareness, revealing who we really are, releasing all that stuff that no longer serves us and stands in the light of our own true authentic self.

"Sometimes we may be guided to take certain steps to shift our energies and perspective and move into a new vibration. Our subconscious is impressed by feelings, energy and passion. When we speak or write a treatment, we need to feel it. Our subconscious cannot tell the difference between an image vividly entertained and an actual experience. If we embody the vision and experience it in our imagination, as far as our subconscious is concerned, it is reality.

"This conference is all about anchoring a new frequency of awareness that we may embrace day by day in our everyday lives. When you wake in the morning, start the day with a new thought. Affirm, 'I am divine potential unfolding. I live in the midst of divine abundance. My highest vision is unfolding for me now. I am seeing love all around me. I live in a friendly universe.' And then, with this knowing feeling, move into your day on a higher frequency. Start the day with energy and enthusiasm.

"Separate yourself from gossip and complaining. Excuse yourself from negative conversations. Be aware of what you are attracting into your life. It's all about maintaining the frequency. Do some forgiveness work: who, in your life, may now be released and forgiven? The true spirit of you can rise above whatever may have happened. Love yourself enough to set yourself free, knowing that holding on to blame and resentment does not serve you. It's time to forgive and let go.

"Make this your best day yet. I challenge you to take on the best-day-yet philosophy. It's up to you. You can be detached from it all and say, 'It's not my best day until it shows up.' But think what creates your day? Are you the creation of your day or do you create it? Be in the presence of your dream. See it, feel it, imagine it, visualise it. Feel the joy and celebration. Imagine yourself in total alignment with your dream. Let your dream unfold and move in the direction of your dreams, act as if they've already come true."

New Thought philosophy is designed
to bring us into self-mastery in every area of our lives.

"I like to take down walls and open hearts," began David Leonard, "and I will take you to that place of vulnerability and authenticity where we get to know our oneness. This is a beautiful opportunity for us to have a direct experience of what is real. And what I do know is that we are all going to get exactly what we need." From southern Alabama, USA, David was charismatic and softly spoken, embracing the audience with his emotive and genuinely open-hearted style.

"There are two kinds of people in this world, those who think they are separate and those who know we are all connected. The gift, the challenge and the opportunity, is to make that discovery for ourselves. Ernest Holmes wrote, 'You must make this discovery for yourself and realise that the thing you are looking for is the thing you are looking with.'

"My invitation to you is to stop seeking and to start finding what is already here. Life gives us exactly what we need. Ultimately, we realise that the outer does not provide happiness. Happiness is an inside job.

"The secret is this: if you can want what you have instead of needing what you want, you will be happy. What if you knew that the very thing you were wanting already exists? The kingdom is within. You already have it. There is nothing to get. What I know for us all is that we are here to have an experience. I call it a dance of awakening. And it takes courage. What I am going to ask you to do is to take down the walls and open the window of your heart. As we experience this, we realise that what we see in others is but a reflection of ourselves. We must be willing to see the face of God in each other. Namaste – the God in me sees the God in you. And in that place, we are one. To me that is where true abundance lies, in the realisation of who we really are. Then the seeking stops, the realisation begins and the dance continues.

"What I have learned is that we are not so much afraid of the unknown as of letting go of the known. We are afraid of letting go of who we think we are, or of what we think we are supposed to know. When we have the courage to step out of the comfort zone and leap into that uncertain place, there is a discovery that is timeless, endless and always happening in the eternal now where there is no past or future. We cannot know what it's going to be. It is the great mystery that is calling us. Dr Roger talked about living your dream and Rumi the poet says, 'Each one of us has come here to do something incredible that only we can do.' We are here to play the game of life, but not necessarily to win it – by playing it, we may discover that it is not meant to be a struggle, it is meant to be a dance."

Thus while Eastern philosophy invites us to explore the path of least resistance, to go with the flow and move effortlessly in the current of life, so David Leonard, full of southern warmth and charm, was suggesting that we enjoy the moment, dance with life and not take ourselves too seriously.

Queues formed around the long tables laden with a sumptuous buffet lunch, to be enjoyed al fresco in the afternoon sunshine on the grass verges surrounding the hotel. It was a real summer picnic and epitomised the whole easy-going, joyful and fun atmosphere of the conference that belied the profundity of the wisdom we had listened to. Then it was back to business and the air-conditioned coolness of the hotel.

Dr Susan Smith Jones was established in the lecture suite and was treating her audience to a workshop entitled Choose to be Healthy and Celebrate Life. Her enthusiasm and passion for her subject was infectious, the workshop already oversubscribed and the room full to capacity. We stopped by to check on proceedings but couldn't find a spare seat. Susan's intimate knowledge and Californian charm was winning over any doubters and everyone now listened attentively, gleaning helpful hints to make life happier, healthier and more fun.

'You are what you eat' was as clear and relevant a message as 'thoughts become things'. (We were relieved that our carefully planned buffet menus were focused on healthy eating.) Susan reminded us that we are holistic beings and that the thoughts we think, the food we eat and the actions we take very much shape who and what we become. Nature provides us with an abundant storehouse of all that we need to lead happy and healthy lives.

We felt blessed to have assembled such an awesome team of speakers and musicians under one roof. There was a diverse programme that was both enlightening and entertaining. While Roger offered us profound wisdom, David appealed to the heart with his afternoon workshop, The Game of Life: How to Use the Spiritual Laws. Susan was fun, knowledgeable and very dedicated, while Michael and Karen provided beautiful and inspiring music. Kathy Hearn, Community Spiritual Leader, added an extra touch of grace with an in-depth history of Science of Mind, The Best-Kept Secret of the Twenty-First Century.

We had embarked on an ambitious journey, an enterprise that was soul deep, our cup filled to overflowing, and now we needed a brief respite to digest all that we had experienced before the evening programme: Dancing With Angels – an Extravaganza of Words and Music.

We had invited a number of outside guests who were unable to attend the whole conference to join us for the evening and get a taste of what we were all about. Smartly dressed for the evening, men in jackets and ties and women in colourful summer dresses, they began to arrive. As the summer sun shone through the windows of the ballroom we sat down to dinner, to be followed by a packed programme of music and talks.

There was music from Michael and Karen, a solo performance from our London-based musician Mark Hughes, and a few surprises. One of our study group members, a gifted actor and singer, gave a beautiful impromptu performance of an operatic classic that evoked a standing ovation and calls for an encore, while his equally talented daughter brought the house down and got tears rolling with a heartfelt version of an Italian love song. There was such an abundance of talent on show that evening that it felt almost dream-like. The sheer depth and quality of Michael's voice as he sang *Spirit in Me* was a privilege to experience, while Karen's self-penned classic *The Face of God* moved many to tears before she concluded her set with the gentle *Beloved*, a tribute to her dear friend and our next speaker, David Leonard.

David was a bundle of loving energy. Trained as a dancer and brought up in the performing arts, his talks never lacked drama or emotional intensity. We wondered whether he would perhaps be a trifle too intense for our audience, but the truth was they loved him. He was honest and open and wore his heart on his sleeve, and the title of his talk that evening was, appropriately, End the Struggle and Dance with Life (borrowed from Susan Jeffers' best-selling book).

"Dance, for me, was natural and instinctive," he began, "but there were times when things might go wrong. And when things go wrong you just have to lighten up and not take it too seriously, because more often than not the audience do not even notice. You have to discover the secret for yourself. You have to discover how to set yourself free from any self-imposed nonsense. I have a tee-shirt at home that says, 'Life is too mysterious to be serious'.

"Life is a beautiful dance waiting to be danced, something to be discovered but not invented. We've touched on some really heavy stuff today and several people have come up to me after my workshop and told me about their break-outs and breakthroughs. It's just how you may choose to frame it. I like to bless things as they happen and reveal the deeper truths through stories. The great teacher Jesus spoke in stories and parables. Life itself is a story. But it is only when we get into life that we discover how to fully participate in the dance.

"End the struggle and dance with life. But before we can end the struggle," David suggested, "we must first identify what the struggle is. When I first moved to Huntsville, Alabama, I quickly learned that the law of attraction is always operating. I learned that if you don't deal with and heal your own stuff, you will just attract more of it. If you are a people pleaser, as I was then, and a perfectionist, as I am now, you will attract people like yourself because life is a mirror reflecting back to us who we are.

"I once attracted a lady who came to me with a whole shopping list of problems, which she talked about in such detail and with such energy that at the end of the day I said to her, 'If you argue so strongly for your limitations, they will become yours.' I don't think that's what she wanted to hear and strangely enough I didn't see her again. For a while I continued to attract similar people until I learned that life gives you exactly what you need. But you can take what life gives you and turn it into some kind of blessing.

"There is a little part of me, however, that still thinks that I have to impress people. I confess to being a perfectionist with a host of inner critics. I don't have just one critic, I have a whole committee and they usually convene in the middle of the night. But what I have learned is that I have to embrace my inner critics and invite them in, not try and get rid of them. They are all a part of me and at the strangest moment they will come knocking at my door. The truth is that they are here to help and I've learned to integrate all parts of me, not just the parts I love – the creative, spontaneous, sweet and loving parts – but also the fearful, worried, crazy, insecure parts of me that I really don't want anybody to see. So how, you may ask, do we overcome the struggle and learn to dance with life? Well, we each have to discover that for ourselves.

"In Science of Mind we teach that there is a power in the universe greater than us that we can use. But what we fail to realise about the power is that… we are it. When we think we can control it, direct it, manipulate it – in that very attempt we only limit it. Life really is a beautiful dance waiting to be danced, something to be discovered but not invented.

"When I first took up my ministry I recall saying to the universe, 'Please, take me anywhere but Alabama.' I realised that the universe has a quaint sense of humour. So, it took me to Alabama. Having decided that I was not going to struggle, I had to experience struggle.

"Several people have shared with me about feelings that had come up that they didn't know what to do with, feelings of sadness or unworthiness, feelings of fear of intimacy or of being hurt. I said, 'What if you could just allow the space for those feelings to arise?' By creating a space for these feelings you are not under their power. By resisting them you allow them to have power over you. We are all engaged in this dance of life and we tend to get exactly what we need. The beautiful thing about the law of attraction is that it is always operating in its fullness and when we let go of struggle we may receive the most beautiful blessings.

"A couple of years ago, I was invited to a conference in Jamaica. At the last minute the conference was cancelled but I didn't want to alter my plans so I thought I would take time off instead and have a little retreat in the mountains with some friends. At the time I was still grieving the loss of my pet dogs. They had got old and sick and had both passed at the same time. My partner was too upset to think about getting another dog and I was feeling the loss badly too. It was like my family and I missed them. 'Maybe I should get another dog,' I thought. 'But you want the perfect dog', my partner responded. 'For you it has to be the perfect dog. It can't be a puppy, it has to be housetrained and so it has to be an older dog. It has to be short-haired because long-haired dogs are too much to look after. In short it has to be perfect.' And so we had this mental equivalent of a dog that was almost impossible. We wanted a saint for a dog.

"Anyway, while we were up in the mountains we came across this old dog with spots on his nose and white patches on his paws and tail and we called him Speck. Every morning at the crack of dawn he would come to the cabin where we were staying and would wait patiently outside the door while I was in meditation, and when I got up he would accompany me for long walks. He was so quiet, he was magic and I soon fell in love with Speck. I told my friends, 'I want a dog like Speck. Do you suppose I can take him home?' 'Of course not,' they replied, 'he belongs here.' So I just let it go.

"One Sunday afternoon some time later we were driving through the mountains in Georgia. Everything was closed but my friends had noticed a sign on the side of the road saying Humane Society, and there were little paw prints leading up the mountain road. They said, 'Let's go up there and see the animals.' I said, 'I don't want to go and see animals cooped up in a pound. It depresses me to see the cats and dogs in the cages.' They said, 'Well David, why don't you just go up there and open your heart to them?' 'But,' I argued, insisting, 'this is my weekend off and I don't want to go.'

"I was outnumbered however, two against one, and before I knew it we were heading up this mountain following the painted paw prints even though I was still resisting. Well, we got to the top and it was closed. One of my friends got out of the car and knocked on the door. It turned out that they were cleaning the place. He enquired, 'Would you mind if we came in and just had a look at the animals?' They opened the doors and rather reluctantly I walked in. But when I saw those beautiful cats I must admit my heart started to open.

"'Let's take a look at the puppy pound,' suggested my friend. 'I am not going in there,' I insisted. 'Oh, come on,' they said. So, I went into the puppy cage as they were hosing down all the poop and stuff. All the little dogs were barking and the next thing I heard was my friend saying, 'Oh my God, it's a baby Speck.' And there in the cage sitting quite Zen-like was this tiny little puppy with speckles on his nose and tail and four white paws. My friend then stepped into the cage over all the poop and stuff, picked up the tiny puppy and thrust her into my arms. 'Here she is. It's your demonstration!'

"And I said, 'Huh?' 'You've got to take her,' he said, 'you asked for her and the Lord has given her to you.' 'But she's a puppy,' I replied, 'and that was one of the rules, remember?' 'Well, she's short-haired and she doesn't bark. She's a Zen dog.' So I said, 'Well, we can't have her.' You know how the mind works. 'We can't get her because… it's a Sunday and the pound is officially closed.' My friend enquired, 'Can this man buy this dog?' The attendant replied, 'Well, she has been spayed and today is her adoption day. Do you have eighty dollars?' I just happened to have five twenty-dollar bills in my wallet and, still in a state of shock, handed eighty dollars over to the attendant who then handed me baby Speck. We went back down the mountain and I called my partner. 'Guess what?' I said, 'We've got a dog.'

"So the universe gives you things when you least expect it. In a strange sort of way, the very thing you resist most comes to you and opens your heart. Now I have baby Speck and baby Bert. They are friends and when I come home at night they both come running down the stairs to greet me. They will sit at the foot of my chair while I pick a toy from their toy box, which they will play with in a sort of friendly tug-of-war. Fascinated, I will sit and watch them for an hour or so while time seems to stand still. Life gives you so many sweet blessings in amazing disguises when you simply stop struggling and dance with life."

The intensity of the conference, as we began to realise, had accelerated our spiritual growth and understanding out of all proportion to the short time we had spent together, taking things further and deeper than we'd ever been before. Linda and I were so grateful that we had accepted 'the invitation'.

"Whatever we are grateful for," said Dr Kathy Hearn as she invoked the final blessing of the day, "we increase.

"While we talk about living in the presence, we seem to spend so much time focusing on what we don't have. We cannot create presence out of absence. So let's take time out to complete this day in a state of gratitude. Let us scroll through the day from the very beginning, the wonderful talks, the music and workshops, the breaks and mealtimes we have spent together and this evening's enlightening entertainment.

"And as we review the day, what stands out for us? What has been particularly meaningful? Was it something we may have heard for the first time, an 'Aha' moment, a realisation or maybe a breakthrough at the level of the heart? Whatever it might be, let's identify the one thing that was most meaningful, most important and hold it in our consciousness. What was the greater realisation that we have had? What have we learned and what was the greater idea of Spirit that may have opened our eyes and minds in a way we have never known before? So let's just be grateful for being here, for engaging in this day. Let's thank our higher wisdom self and share our experience of this day in gratitude.

"We are grateful for this hotel, for the wonderful food we have enjoyed today, for Mother Earth for producing it and for all the hands that have helped prepare it. And most of all we give thanks to Spirit for the activity of the One, the One life of all beings everywhere, the activity of the One that is guiding us now, the One that is love beyond all measure that we only know by our faith, the One that guides and directs our every step, the One that takes us absolutely to our highest good. In faith and joy and love, we call this day complete. We call it good, in fact very good and together we say, 'And so it is.'"

To the sound of Karen Drucker singing *I Am So Grateful*, the day came to a close. Profound connections had been made, new friendships forged and, for some, conversation would linger long into the early hours. For others it was a time of quiet reflection. For Linda and me it was the end of a perfect day, a breathtaking rollercoaster ride that had begun at six in the morning and danced deliriously until the lights dimmed and the curtains were drawn. We were happy and satisfied that all had gone perfectly to plan and, in some ways, even better than expected. As we anticipated the day ahead, Karen and Michael's song played in our heads.

'There is only love, love that heals, love that sets us free, there is only love…'

David and Linda open the Abundant Living Conference

Dr Roger Teal

The Power of Prayer

The beauty of a two-day event was that everything was very focused and compact and yet there was still time to develop relationships and delve a little deeper. As Linda and I prepared to introduce the second day's programme, we could feel a wave of warm, loving energy. Our weekend community had become like a family, all eager to go a little deeper and embrace the unique quality of love and healing that pervaded the conference. The morning music from Karen and Michael invited us to *Shine our Light and Be Open to the World*. Then our keynote speaker for the day, Dr Roger Teel, took to the stage and immediately acknowledged the palpable shift of energy.

"The energetic transformation from yesterday morning to today has been quite profound and beautiful," he began, "and it is wonderful to be a part of it and for there to be such receptivity."

Dr Roger's talk was about the nature of prayer and of God. Traditionally, people have beseeched a distant, detached deity, but in Science of Mind prayer is intended to facilitate a shift in our own consciousness and we begin to see God in a new light.

There are many interesting interpretations as to the nature of God, apart from that of the Bible. The Native American Indians refer simply to the Great Spirit, an overriding benevolent power and presence that infuses all living things with its beauty and essence. New Thought talks about a Power for Good in the universe greater than us, that we can use. In the words of musician Daniel Nahmoud's classic anthem, 'There's one power invisible and you see it everywhere and every day. One power indescribable and you speak of it with every word you say.'

When we contemplate the miracle of life, the vastness of space, the ever expanding universe and the infinity of time, God makes sense and completes the mystery of the cosmic jigsaw. The point of affirmative prayer, or spiritual mind treatment, is that we not only have a personal relationship with the one power – acknowledging its presence in, through and around all things and all people – but we can use this power to enrich and enhance our lives and the lives of those around us. What really matters is the state of our own consciousness.

Ernest Holmes said, 'Affirmative prayer is not something we do to another, to an environment or a situation. It is always the thing we do to ourselves. It is an action in thought that expands the consciousness, provides clarity of mind, removes the obstructions of thought and lets in the light.'

"For me the experience of prayer is like a spiritual homecoming," Dr Roger continued. "Dr Holmes says, 'There is a time when we enter into prayer when we must turn from the condition, otherwise the prayer just becomes animated by the energy of the problem itself.' Sometimes we just have to let go. Sometimes we may think the only way to extricate ourselves from a situation is to hate it. But what we hate, we energise, and it will continue to persist. We have to start loving the situations, blessing the people involved and knowing that the situation is being transformed. And sometimes we learn that what really needs healing is ourselves!

"If we can learn to love where we are, life can lead us to where we want to be. Emmet Fox, the great metaphysician says, 'We are always in our right place. The right place is always where we are.' It might not seem like it and we might resist it, but if we resist what is going on, we only give it more power. There is a power in blessing where we are.

"Prayer works through our own consciousness. It cannot work if our energies are full of hate and remorse. This has to shift before the bigger idea can be realised. Prayer can heal and transform our consciousness without expecting or needing conditions to change, understanding that the right guidance will be there for us to move forward. Conditions will shift as and when necessary. We tend to think it is something out there that needs to shift, but in fact it is something within us that shifts in true prayer, with the realisation that nothing is withheld, nothing is missing in terms of the divine. And that is what we have to heal within ourselves.

"Affirmative prayer brings us into an enlightened space where we are not praying to change our experience, we are praying to open to the truth of who we really are for our highest good." Roger paused for a moment, reflecting on a time in his own life when the power of prayer came to the fore in a most remarkable way.

"I would like to share an experience that happened to me when I was a young, novice minister at my first church in Portland, Oregon, in the mid-1970s. There was a small group of us at the time, about twenty-five in all, and we held our meetings at a local rented hall. Gradually our numbers grew and before long we were nearly a hundred. The hall we were using was about to close and so we had to find alternative accommodation. Knowing there was a right place for us, we started to look around.

"While I was away on vacation, I received a 'phone call from one of our members saying she had found an old church that needed renovation but was available for two hundred thousand dollars. It was a five hundred seater church and with a down payment of eighty thousand dollars we could have it. We had barely a hundred members. It was a very ambitious target and raising eighty thousand dollars in time was a tall order. We had only a month to do it or the deal was off. I asked my members, 'Do you believe we can do it?' and they replied, 'We believe if you believe.' And I said, 'Well, I am working on that.'

"We started fundraising of every imaginable kind and after three weeks, amazingly, we had raised sixty thousand dollars. But here I was, their spiritual leader, realising that we were still twenty thousand dollars short of our target. The owner had allowed us to occupy the premises temporarily. We had moved in as much as we could and I had set up my office. We had really made ourselves at home. But without the required down payment we would have to leave our new home by the next week. I was in deep struggle. What was I going to tell these people? Everybody had been incredible, but I feared it was not going to work. We had only three or four more days. That coming Sunday would be our last Sunday and we would have to be out by the following Wednesday. What were we going to do?

"I was in angst and finally suggested, 'Maybe we ought to pray about this?' And so I stilled my mind and entered into prayer. Sometimes in prayer we are not praying to change an experience, we are just praying to open to the truth and the realisation of the highest good.

"Through prayer, I found new insight into how best to lead in this situation. All of a sudden, I began to see these people, my community, in a new light – this little band of people who had barely known the teaching when I first arrived just eighteen months earlier, who had followed me even though I didn't know where I was going or what I was doing. But we had a dream and they loved what we were about so much that they were willing to pool their resources at such short notice and in such a short space of time to the tune of sixty thousand dollars, which back in those days was a lot of money!

"I didn't want to focus on the fact that we were twenty thousand dollars short. I just wanted to celebrate their incredible achievement and manifestation of love. All of a sudden, tears started to roll down my cheeks at the truth of these people and the beauty they had manifested. And then I realised there was the answer. We were winners! It didn't matter if this place was not to be our home. It didn't matter because we had knitted together as a community. There was a new energy around. New people were showing up. There was a vibrancy and excitement. All that we had accomplished, it was holy work and I knew exactly what I was going to say to them on that final Sunday.

"I told them, 'I don't want any long faces because we are going to be moving out of this place the coming week. But I tell you something – we are winners! Look at what we've done. Look at how we are loving each other. Look at the kind of community we have become. We are walking in the Spirit and we are going to take that sixty thousand dollars and Spirit will guide us to exactly what is for our highest and best. We are the miracle and it is happening now.'

"Everyone was on their feet clapping and cheering. It was a beautiful moment and the most wonderful feeling. Well, the next day I thought I would get a head start and pack up all my boxes and church equipment as we had to be out by the Wednesday. I needed to clear my office so I got some boxes and went to the back door of my office when I noticed an envelope laying on the floor. I didn't know what it was so I put my boxes down and picked up the envelope. And when I opened it, it took my breath away. Inside the envelope was a cheque for twenty thousand dollars from an unnamed donor! I stood in stunned amazement at this incredible, unexpected blessing that had come our way. To this day, I have never found out who the anonymous donor was who had saved the day with that timely additional funding.

"I realised then that we had moved out of limitation and into the fullness of manifestation and, you know what, I had released that building. Sometimes you just have to let something go and, if it comes back to you, you know it's right. Maybe I would have been happy to have moved on and be guided to somewhere else. But we had our home

in that beautiful building and spent weekend after weekend trans-
forming it over the next two years, deepening and growing as we did.

"Prayer provides a wonderful opportunity to explore the magic and
mystery of the universe. It's also about spiritual homecoming, about
letting the power unfold in, through and as us.

"Dr Holmes says, 'Pray until you get results.' He believed in regular
prayer. Some people suggest that our first prayer, or treatment, plants
the seed deep in the divine soil, in the law, so that we don't need any
further prayers. I find that our ongoing prayers serve to keep us in the
consciousness, but we need to be anchored there.

"Regular daily prayer is one way to weed the garden of doubts,
understanding that doubts are just old thinking trying to reassert itself.
We may have established a new vibration of thinking, but our old ways
don't just pack their bags and head for the highway, they keep trying to
reassert themselves. The occasional weed will not destroy the garden,
but if we leave them and do nothing about them, they will eventually
take over the garden. We need to acknowledge our doubts, then pull
them out and move forward with the vision of our prayer.

"Sometimes, as we go deeper into prayer, old issues and doubts
may surface. Sometimes these recurring doubts may uncover aspects
of our consciousness that need to be healed – the fear, guilt, blame,
etcetera – anything that may not be in alignment with our forward
growth. Things come up. Thoughts arise which may not be congruent
with the new space we are energising in our prayer work. It can be
empowering to embrace them, but never to judge ourselves as not
being enough."

Roger concluded his talk with an invitation and a challenge.

"The work we are all involved in takes courage. It is blessed work,
but we are never alone. 'Where two or more are gathered, I will be
there.' We must seek to find our spiritual community. We must remember who we are, to know we are not alone, that there is always love and
support just as we have generated and experienced here over the last

few days. And it's through prayer we may not only explore the magic and mystery of the universe, we may also find our own true spiritual homecoming."

We are not praying to change our experience,
we are praying to open to the truth
of who we really are for our highest good.

"I am going to make this talk short, sweet and very juicy," promised David Leonard, our next speaker. "I am going to tell you about the meaning of life in thirty minutes. But, you know what, I don't have the answer either for you or for me.

"What I do know is that life for me is all about one thing, love. When we open to and allow love to flow from our hearts, and cease trying to judge one another, then all we need is love. Love is all we need. In the Science of Mind teaching it says, 'Let love lead the way and we will find love everywhere, because love is what we are.'

"Life actually is a metaphor. It is constantly teaching us, preaching to us and giving us a message to be present, to experience the moment, to listen with our heart and to give and receive love. In the words of Karen and Michael's beautiful song, 'There is only love, love that heals, love that sets us free, there is only love.' We need to love and accept people for who and what they are. We are not here to fix someone else's problems. What needs to shift is the consciousness of the individual. We need to love and accept what is before we can move on to what we may become.

"We are not here to fix the problem, we are here to hold that space in consciousness, to love people where they are, to know that when conditions are right within them, they will shift. But there is something within us that makes us think we need to change the other person, that there is something wrong with them. But we just need to be there for them, to love them for who they are and for what they may become.

"There is a lovely saying, 'Birds sing not because they have a message, but because they have a song.' And the Buddhists say, 'Compassion, like the fragrance of the flower once the bud has opened, is the highest form of love.' Ernest Holmes said, 'The thing you are looking for is the thing you are looking with.' The love you are seeking is already seeking you.

"There is no power like love and I just want to tell you that when you leave here you will be infectious. You will infect the world with your love. The invitation, then, is just to listen, to surrender, to allow what is really calling you, to leave what may be someone else's dream for your life and to find your own dream. The philosopher Henry David Thoreau said, 'I don't want to find that I have lived someone else's version of my life.' So, let us have the courage to live deliberately, to discover that which is calling us to our greatness and to know that it is love that will take us there."

There was an undeniable energy of love at the conference now that was difficult to describe, a feeling of connection, belonging and shared spiritual purpose.

"Love is where we came from," echoed Dr Kathy Hearn, bringing the morning session to a close, "and love is where we are going, what we are here for and what it's all about while we are here.

"If we want more love in our life, we have to make room for it. When our consciousness shifts and we have new thoughts, new ideas about life, about Spirit and our possibilities, we begin to release the bonds that bind us to the way things have been. Things begin to fall away, but that is part of the process. And if we are really courageous we can understand that the falling away is an important part of the cycle when a new birth may take place. If we want a greater expression of love in our life, we need to become more loving, become aware of any fear or resistance we may have to being truly open and present with someone else. Because love is all there is and it is love that will shift us into a new spiral of consciousness that will ultimately change the planet."

Love is where we came from
and love is where we are going, what we are here for.

Planetary transformation would have to wait, however, because it was time for lunch: mouth-watering salads and delicacies, exotic fruits and patterned plates of mozzarella, avocado and beef tomatoes. Who said healthy eating could not look and taste amazing?

It was an appropriate entrée for Dr Susan Smith Jones' afternoon workshop, with even more food for thought and intriguing insights from her own personal practice and experience. Her message was simple and clear: Love Yourself, Look after Your Body and Live Life to the Full. Susan was a shining example of someone who has faced life's challenges head on and come through with stories to tell, lessons to learn and empowering experiences to share.

Elsewhere, David Leonard invited his audience to Feel the Fear and Do It Anyway (courtesy of Susan Jeffers). He too was a past master at dealing with life's slings and arrows and to come out the other side still smiling, still loving and with faith intact. What made David and his talks so popular was that he talked from the heart and was willing to bare his soul with disarming honesty.

For the final talk of the day, Dr Roger Teel offered us a Spiritual Takeaway – Tools and Tips for Positive Change. It felt like we had been transported into a metaphysical time warp where daily life had seemed to stand still. But as the minutes ticked by towards the inevitable conclusion of this life-changing weekend, we needed some practical advice – and a reminder that we had changed and, fortunately, that life would never be quite the same again.

"My heart is so full of this incredible conference," he began, "and all that we have experienced and created together this weekend. We have experienced the real world here and now we are going back into the world of unreality. But we shall leave here empowered by this experience and we shall have to be clear how we are going to express it in the way that serves us best.

"I invite us to go forth from here reinventing ourselves, knowing that life supports us and that we don't have to march to the beat of another's drum. We can do it our way. We can live in a new reality that maintains we are all one, that we are all unfolding as an embodiment of love and truth. Regardless of the outcome, Spirit holds us kindly. The universe does not hold up a score card when we take a leap. There is no judgment. The universe simply says, 'I knew you could do it. You deserve the best.'

"We can have our jump time. We can leap forward into life projecting this beautiful energy and consciousness, understanding that life loves us regardless of how things turn out. As we move back into the unreal world, I invite us to consider that the way things worked before doesn't have to be the way they work now. We can bring new energy and light into those areas of our lives that we may have given up on and create the opportunity for true transformation. Life never gives up on us, if we don't give up on it.

"Ghandi said, 'Let us be the change we want to see in the world.' To be the change we want to see in our own lives, we must maintain and activate change every day and remind ourselves of who we really are, of the love that is centred right here, and bring that gift back into the world.

"Ernest Holmes said, 'Life has need of us, or we would not be here.' Spirit has need of us or it would not have infused us with life. We must know that new ways of consciousness need to be anchored in being, or old thoughts will simply reclaim their place and pull us back into old ways.

"A lot has been spoken and talked about this weekend, but there are times when we must withdraw into the silence with our hearts open. After a conference like this, it is invaluable to find time to be still, to be with the energy, because everything we have talked about is really beyond words. Many mystical teachers have struggled to express their larger perception of life through the limited confines of language. What they may have experienced at first hand was so much beyond what words alone can convey.

"To fully describe the wealth of information we have experienced this weekend, we need time to be quiet. When we are in the silence, in the presence of the divine, we begin to notice that every moment mirrors the face of God, every experience offers manifold blessings. In time, something extraordinary wells up within us and infiltrates our prayer work and lifts us to a greater dimension of being. And this knowingness is only gained in the silence, in periods of stillness. So let us be the change we want to see in the world, practise stillness and kindness and shine our light so brightly for everyone to see."

Life has need of us, or we would not be here.

Dr Kathy Hearn picked up the theme with typical grace and brought the conference to a close with a final benediction.

"We are like shards of light," she began, "seeded in a new consciousness, radiating out into the world. I would like to thank everyone for their participation and presence here this weekend, for those of us who have come from far away, who have tasted the food and breathed the air of England. We are one.

"We have talked about the re-entry process, readapting to the unreal world. When we are in this consciousness, it is a rarefied atmosphere and when we re-enter the world we will have changed. We may never know the power that may emanate from our practices, from our words and thoughts and how they may affect other people. We are all connected. Staying connected is all about staying connected to God, to Spirit and to one another. Separation is an illusion. To come back to the truth of oneness we need to have people around us who can remind us who we really are. It's all about connection and community.

"It is my heartfelt desire and highest intention for us all to continue engaging with this wonderful teaching of New Thought and Science of Mind. In the words of the poet Rumi, 'Out beyond all ideas of right and wrong there is a field, I will meet you there. When the soul lies down in the grass, the world is too full to think about ideas, thoughts or the phrase 'each other'. It doesn't' make sense.'

"Sometimes people may feel isolated, separated and disconnected. But we cannot be separate from God, from the One. We may think we are, we may feel that we are, we may tell ourselves that we are, but it is not the truth. I invite us all to find a way to connect with similar like-minded people. There is great value in being in a group, coming together in spiritual community. I could not have advanced in my life without the love, support and challenge of my community.

"Recently I attended the Parliament of World Religions in Barcelona, representing The Association of Global New Thought. With all the different traditions, practices and types of prayer on offer, my experience of it was that whilst we were all different, we were all one. Despite the costumes, cultures and rituals that might mark us out as different, we are all essentially connected. We may visit sacred places, the churches, temples, synagogues and mosques, where people may have different names for God. But it doesn't really matter as long as the one power and presence is being respected and acknowledged.

"When we connect with our tribe, with those similar others who are engaged in this work, we create a sacred space and feel the name of God being spoken in the way most meaningful for us. I welcome the opportunity we have had this weekend to be together, to breathe the same air, to tread the same path and to be truly connected in love."

'We all need a prayer to remind us who we are…' The words and melody of Michael's hauntingly beautiful song sent shivers down my spine and summed up the mood, the feeling and the profound connections we had all experienced that weekend. The music had been an outstanding feature of the conference. Far from being an enjoyable interlude between the talks, the music had acted as a bridge, linking themes, complementing ideas and presenting powerful affirmations. To have such a brilliant trio of musical talent as Michael, Karen and Mark had been a real blessing and had added a depth of colour warmth and sensitivity to proceedings.

'Come together and let's create a celebration of life…' sang Mark. Hundreds had indeed come together from all ends of the country and far beyond to celebrate and forge a conference to remember, a joyful, healing, uplifting and enlightening experience. But soon it would be time to leave.

"Hold on," implored our esteemed keynote speaker, Dr Roger Teel. "Let's hold hands and visualise ourselves heading home from this place imparting the kindness we have talked about, basking in this wonderful feeling, this thing called life, this thing called love. Let's bless this whole experience and imagine the weeks and months ahead unfolding with the new consciousness we have acquired to anchor ourselves in this truth. Imagine a great light kindled in our hearts, emanating out into the world. Dr Holmes said, 'If we could see a spiritual mind treatment, we would see it as a beam of light.'

"A great light is emanating out from this place, from the energy and vibration we have created. It will not fade when we leave. It is anchored in our hearts and will continue to shine over the coming weeks and months, animated and empowered by this experience. I bless each and every one as we look around and behold the beautiful souls who have co-created this experience – the speakers and musicians, those who have planned and organised this incredible event, and those who have come from far and wide to be here."

A sudden beam of sunlight danced through the half-drawn curtains, illuminating the faces of our assembled gathering, our weekend community. For a magical moment it seemed like the whole room was bathed in light as Karen sang a plaintive prayer for peace to round off proceedings.

Let there be peace – I stand for peace.
Let there be joy – I stand for joy.
Let there be love – I stand for love.
We are making a new world now.

And so it was that the 2009 UK New Thought Conference for Abundant Living came to a close. For two extraordinary days we had been living in a spiritual dreamland, delightfully detached from the outside unreal world, experiencing true spiritual connection and community. Now it was time to transpose all we had learned into a language the outside world could comprehend.

This unique event and particular combination of people would never be repeated, although the ripples from the conference would continue to spread, touching souls along the way for months, even years to come, with future events and conferences from Bournemouth to Geneva.

"I want to come back," pleaded one musician. "Please invite me again."

"If I had known how good it would be," confessed one guest, "I would have told all my friends to come."

As people headed for home, hotels and airports, amidst heartfelt hugs and handshakes, Linda and I stood back to enjoy a moment of pride and satisfaction with a job well done, a mission completed, a vision realised. To be honest, by the time we had bade farewell to our final few guests we were exhausted, in a good way, thankful that everything had gone even better than expected, and wondering what Spirit might have in store for us next...

We had enjoyed every moment, every talk, workshop and carefully planned performance, as well as the refreshingly spontaneous deviations from the script. We had been blessed with beautiful weather; the hotel, speakers and musicians had excelled and we had been nourished by delicious food and spiritual wisdom. We had made a host of new friends and were overwhelmed by the flood of emails, texts and letters that came our way.

> *"The energy, the music, the speakers – it's been inspirational and energising. I feel so energised and alive! I've not felt so good for quite some time. It's an amazing feeling. I enjoyed the 2007 conference, but following this year's think I now get it." KB*

> *"Every day, every hour, every minute and every second was magical! Thank you both from the bottom of my heart, which is still so full of love, light and gratitude." MC*

> *"Fantastic motivational talks and workshops. Thank you so much for organising a wonderful weekend. So much love had gone into it that was truly felt and appreciated." LJ*

> *"The speakers were all extraordinary as was the music and the movement between the two contributed to the amazing energy and experience of elevated consciousness." BL*

> *"I took something from every talk and song that was shared with us. The people who attended have now become my family. I was nourished and cleansed from this experience. Thank you." NF*

It was gratifying to receive these and many more positive, life-affirming acknowledgments of appreciation, as well as a kind email from Dr Roger Teel. "Congratulations," he began, "on the creation and delivery of a valuable, meaningful and inspirational conference of real substance and spiritual power. I am certain that those who were truly open and willing were greatly blessed and that the blessings will continue to unfold for them as the conference consciousness and tools ripple forth into their lives on an ongoing basis. I trust you are allowing yourself to bask in the glow of a tremendous accomplishment in service to Spirit and so many lives."

The Unexpected

The glorious heatwave of June had subsided into a beautifully warm and sunny, summery July. We were not yet ready to immerse ourselves in the unreal world and the idea of another trip to California to catch up with our friends at Asilomar was appealing. This was by now a familiar routine, but this time there would be an unexpected twist. As we arrived at the busy Reception, laden with luggage and late lunch bags, we sensed there was something special in the air.

Our curiosity had been aroused by the sight of a fleet of mobile film units outside – vans, booms, microphones and lighting equipment, together with film crews, directors and producers. A movie was in the making, but what was it all about and who was in it? Rumours abounded (someone said they saw Louise Hay wandering around the grounds) but a casual conversation with one of the cameramen revealed that they were filming a movie produced by none other than Dr Wayne Dyer, one of the most highly respected spiritual teachers of the age.

The movie entitled *The Shift* (originally, *From Ambition to Meaning*), was about a group of people from diverse backgrounds and circumstances, drawn together at a spiritual retreat to find themselves and discover their true life purpose. Ironically, it was a film about a spiritual conference being filmed at a spiritual conference. We were even invited to be extras in one scene and on more than one occasion we almost ended up going into the wrong conference. As the week unfolded, the two conferences seemed to merge together anyway, as though by some strange magnetic force. We gathered in Merrill Hall for an evening talk and entertainment to find some of the stars of the movie sitting in the front row, among them Portia de Rossi accompanied by Ellen DeGeneres.

"Who would you really like to see here as a guest speaker?" a member of staff asked us.

"How about Wayne Dyer?" we responded.

"Sorry, I don't think we could afford him," he smiled. Well…

Apparently, the guest speaker for the evening had been unavoidably delayed and a last minute replacement had to be found. A ripple of disquiet spread amongst the audience before it was announced that a young, novice speaker was about to take to the stage, so would we be patient and forbearing as they might be a little nervous. With nearly a thousand people present, it was indeed a challenging occasion for a novice speaker.

Then the music stopped, the chatter ceased and the curtains were drawn back to reveal the smiling face of none other than Dr Wayne Dyer himself! A wave of laughter and anticipation spread through the audience at this unexpected treat. Dr Dyer introduced himself and explained he had wanted to say a few words about the movie he was making and apologise for any inconvenience or disruption it might have caused.

His wit, warmth and wisdom were legendary, as were his distinctive tone of voice and dry sense of humour. Within minutes he had the audience on the edge of our seats, urging him to continue, and he needed little encouragement. That brief talk, scheduled to last five minutes, extended to over an hour and a half, a metaphysical master-class flowing with spiritual wisdom, insight and humour.

Wayne Dyer talked in his inimitable way about his life, his home in Maui and his family, of whom he was immensely proud, and more specifically of how his life had undergone a seismic shift, a spiritual transformation. He was now more interested in giving than receiving, both in terms of his spiritual wisdom and experience and even of his material wealth. He could have carried on all night, but eventually the original guest speaker arrived, apologised, and thanked Dr Dyer profusely for standing in so brilliantly.

Divine providence? In normal circumstances they would never have been able to book (or afford) Wayne Dyer as a special guest speaker. But by a subtle twist of fate in a unique set of circumstances, here he was addressing the Asilomar Conference as a gesture of goodwill.

Wayne Dyer was a prolific writer and hugely popular speaker, famous for many clever sayings and anecdotes, and there was one simple but true statement of his that we shall always remember and cherish:

Sometimes it's better to be kind than to be right.

In 2015, we would be shocked and saddened to hear of his sudden and untimely transition. We can still see his broad smile and hear his voice, and feel sure that he continues his wonderful work for Spirit in the spirit world.

In early February, 2010, the postman knocked twice and with an insistence that demanded response. We opened the door to be greeted by a friendly smile and a heavy brown package, postmarked Arizona, USA.

"Looks interesting," the postman commented with obvious curiosity, as we signed for the unexpected arrival. Carefully we removed the thick brown paper to reveal a beautiful, expertly carved wooden plaque with a stunning border of turquoise stones. The inscription read, 'The International New Thought Alliance presents the Mary Horgan District President's Award to David & Linda Serlin in honor of their commitment to INTA in generating togetherness among New Thought leaders and students'.

The accompanying letter explained that we had been nominated to receive an award for notable activity in promoting and publicising the principles and ideas of New Thought in the UK, an unexpected honour. We had also been invited, all expenses paid, to attend the International New Thought Alliance annual congress in Florida this year and share a dinner table with the President and CEO, Dr Blaine C Mays.

The INTA was highly regarded for its work in bringing together the various strands of New Thought, promoting a wider awareness and understanding of its key principles of peace, unity and prosperity for all.

The New Thought Movement had been founded in the late nineteenth century by a group of eminent, forward-thinking philosophers (amongst them Ralph Waldo Emerson and Henry Thoreau) who dared to challenge the accepted precepts, dogmas and prejudices of the day. Despite the rigidity of prevailing doctrines, it was an exciting and fertile time for flourishing new ideas. New Thought was part of an upsurge of interest in metaphysics, in mental science and in healing, although it owed its true origin to the Bible and to the mystical teachings of the great prophets. Handed down through the ages, encoded in clues and inscribed on parchment such as the Dead Sea scrolls, these fundamental teachings were expressed with profound simplicity by the Master Teacher, for example, as, 'Do unto others as you would have them do unto you.'

New Thought began as a healing movement, synthesising the power of prayer and the omnipresence of Spirit into a powerful formula that helped to heal thousands. Many great names stepped forward to embrace the teachings and blaze a new path, people like Emma Curtis Hopkins, Charles and Myrtle Filmore, Nona Brooks and, of course, Ernest Holmes, the founder of Science of Mind.

All these people seem to have been phenomenal healers with an array of wonderful healings attributed to them. I had grown up seeing healing from a particular perspective, but here was something different that added a whole new dimension to my understanding. It showed me that, ultimately, behind everything there is only one power, a Power for Good.

The main precepts of New Thought were simple:

One life, one mind, one power, one God.
The unity and interconnectedness of all things
and the creative power of thought.
It is done unto you as you believe.

A contemporary definition explains this as, 'A modern spiritual philosophy based on ancient wisdom from the East and West, which affirms the unity of all life and asserts that our thoughts, beliefs and attitudes determine our experience.'

Over time, however, the movement became increasingly intellectualised. More head than heart, some would say. Great minds and worthy thinkers explored the deeper concepts and mystical meanings, yet this only served to overlook the more practical, everyday applications of the teaching.

Then came Ernest Holmes. His enormous passion, zeal and commitment created a whole new teaching structure and subsequently a widespread organisation to disseminate the principles of New Thought to an ever growing audience, making the teachings accessible to everyone. Science of Mind and Spirit was born. Holmes's inspiring words were heard in his popular radio and TV shows in the 1950s (called *This Thing Called Life*), programmes that reached the homes and touched the hearts of millions all over America. People were inspired to take control of their own lives by looking at life from a new perspective, affirming their good through the power of a new kind of prayer.

"There is a Power for Good in the universe greater than we are," he said, "that we can use."

In more recent times, modern metaphysical teachers such as Louise Hay and Wayne Dyer have picked up the baton and expressed their unique versions of the philosophy. The inspirational spiritual leaders Dr Michael Beckwith and Dr Roger Teel, among others, have reinvigorated New Thought and made it accessible to an even wider audience. And the healing dimension, temporarily overlooked, has gradually re-emerged.

In 2006, the book and later film *The Secret* took the media by storm and galvanised enormous popular interest in New Thought principles, key among them being the law of attraction, which has since become almost common vernacular. Napoleon Hill wrote, 'What the mind can conceive and believe, it can achieve.' Quantum mechanics also seems to be confirming the spiritual nature of the universe and that thought affects matter, whilst modern medicine increasingly accepts the role that positive attitude, faith and belief may have in a patient's recovery and wellbeing.

"Expect the best – and get it," wrote acclaimed spiritual minister Dr Norman Vincent Peale, author of *Power of Positive Thinking*.

"You can – if you think you can," echoed wealthy industrialist Henry Ford.

A new kind of philosophy has been reshaping the way we look at life and has proliferated in recent years, with self-help and motivational books filling the bookshop shelves; *The Secret* and Louise Hay's *You Can Heal Your Life* have become bestselling classics. We now live in a world of infinite possibilities where old taboos and traditions are being challenged.

"Now is the appointed time,' wrote metaphysical author Florence Scovel Schinn. "Today is the day of my amazing good fortune. Miracle shall follow miracle and wonders shall never cease."

Discovering New Thought has been wonderful for Linda and me, learning new tools to help us deal more effectively with life's challenges and opportunities. A practical example of this came unexpectedly one Saturday morning at Heathrow's Terminal Four.

We had, we thought, plenty of time to spare as we made our way to the check-in desk for Los Angeles, happy and relaxed as we waited patiently in line. Eventually we stepped forward to be greeted by a smiling clerk who inspected our tickets and passports, then dropped a bombshell.

"Thank you, sir. Now can I see your ESTA?"

What on Earth was that? It had been a few years since we last made a trip to the USA, and apparently there was now a new regulation we hadn't heard of, a compulsory visa-waiver registration.

"No-one told us!" we insisted, in vain of course. No ESTA, no flight. We learned that one has to apply for this form several days before travelling and receive authorisation from the American Embassy within forty-eight hours. We had barely an hour before check-in closed…

Well, anger and indignation, let alone blame, were not going to solve the problem. We sent up simultaneous, silent prayers instead. An immediate answer came from a sympathetic ground crew member who had overheard the conversation.

"You may be able to apply for an ESTA online," he suggested. "There are some computers upstairs. It normally takes two to three days to get authorisation, but if you are very lucky you might just get an immediate response. It's worth a shot."

Having quickly assessed the situation, we realised that time and statistics might be against us but we had a secret weapon up our sleeves, spiritual mind treatment. We would treat and move our feet and give it a go. Calmness and confidence (on the surface anyway) took over where fear and panic had briefly reigned. Linda wheeled the luggage trolley to a quiet corner, got into the zone as best she could and began to treat, quietly affirming 'perfect timing and perfect outcome'. Our son and I rushed upstairs to find the computers – there was just one free. We then discovered that we would need several pound coins, so while I held the fort the boy ran off to get some change. He thought it was all very exciting. I didn't.

I am not a friend of computers but now I was totally focused on finding the right website and downloading the necessary ESTA pages. So far it seemed to be working as I quietly affirmed 'a successful outcome', and somehow I seemed to be guided to find the right things to do. It worked, I was on the right page and now had to answer a host of questions.

Frantically, I filled in the required information, filed my response and waited for the reply. Seconds passed that seemed like minutes and the minutes like hours as the clock on the wall ticked ominously loudly. Then after twenty minutes came back the reply – I had been authorised. I sighed with temporary relief and then started all over again, this time for Linda, speedily repeating the same process. Again the minutes passed relentlessly while the deadline rapidly approached. Linda was authorised, now I had to do the same again for our son, sending out a silent prayer of gratitude that we had allowed plenty of time to spare getting to the airport.

Now we had to get the forms printed off, but there was a queue for the printers and we had run out of change! Everyone around us seemed to be speaking a foreign language, our requests met by blank stares and unsympathetic glances. Off went an excited boy again, to find that pound coins were like gold dust. Eventually he was successful and, exhausted, I filed our documents one by one into the only available, very slow printer. I checked my watch: we had just a couple of minutes to spare.

With the precious papers in hand, we rushed downstairs to find Linda still steadfastly affirming 'perfect timing, perfect outcome'. She looked up anxiously and we smiled in reply, dashing over to the check-in desk just before it closed. The clerk calmly checked our tickets, passports and newly printed (and hard fought) ESTAs, totally unaware of the hair-raising, spine-tingling battle we had just waged – and won, against all odds.

It had been a tight situation, a few minutes more and we would have missed our flight completely. Thank God for the power of treatment. We had proved the power of not accepting 'No' for an answer, of not being deterred by so-called statistics, and above all of realising that Spirit finds a way. As the Virgin jet soared into the afternoon sky, we relaxed at last.

Asilomar had become our personal Mecca. It was not so much what was said, although the speakers were always exceptional, or the workshops, talks and music, which were always inspiring. It was not just the stunning views, the energy of the ocean, the cool dawn mists or piercing midday sunshine. It was not just the intimacy of nature, the deer that would appear unexpectedly at the bedroom window or the raccoons that would pop up cheekily at night. It was the whole thing, the atmosphere of oneness and community, sharing with hundreds of spiritually like-minded people. Just like Stansted Hall had been, it was like coming home. And then we would always return to the UK fired with enthusiasm for new ideas and inspired to get on with some new purpose.

So our happy anticipation was tempered, this year, by the shock news that, after more than fifty historic years, the iconic Asilomar Science of Mind annual conference was soon to be no more. 2011 was its swan song, the final moment of a life-changing event for so many people.

This was the stage where Ernest Holmes himself had delivered so many famous 'sermons by the sea', that had once resonated to rousing talks from countless New Thought giants like Raymond Charles Barker, Donald Curtis, David Walker, Michael Beckwith and Dr Roger Teel, to name but a few. The beautiful, soul-stirring music from the likes of Jami Lula, Michael Gott, Karen Drucker, Robin Hackett and Daniel Nahmoud, that had reverberated through the rafters and moved so many to tears of joy, would no longer echo through this place.

We were disappointed by the news but nonetheless grateful for the many happy times we had enjoyed at this unique retreat by the sea. And, as always, there was a twist in the tale.

It was not by chance, of course, that we reconnected with American-born Reverend Beth Linguri at that final Asilomar conference. We had originally met Beth at one of our UK conferences and she had struck us then as a woman with a mission. Now, she had 'an interesting proposition' for us.

Beth had an imaginative vision for a series of New Thought conferences in the heart of Europe, based in Geneva, with the theme of Conscious Living, Spiritual Awakening, and asked whether we would be interested in participating on the advisory and organising committee. We were naturally delighted and subsequently spent several glorious summers basking in the Swiss sunshine, dining al fresco, mingling with people from all over Europe and enjoying some of the finest current New Thought speakers and musicians. They came largely from the USA and included David Ault, August Gold, Dr John Waterhouse, Dr Kenn Gordon and musical maestro Michael Gott.

With its picture postcard setting and stunning views overlooking Lake Geneva, the Chateau De Bossey, dating back to the fourteenth century, proved to be the perfect healing retreat setting. It was a quite magical place and a far cry from the bustle of LA, the windswept dunes of Asilomar and the leafy lanes of Hertfordshire, England.

From dawn to dusk, the packed three-day programme catered for all aspects of mind, body and spirit and in the evenings, after an open air dinner, there would be music, dance and talks, followed by the inevitable free-flowing discussions with new-found friends. We made many long-lasting friendships at the Geneva conferences, not least Beth herself, who has dedicated so much time and energy in helping to create 'a world that works for everyone'.

In the summer of 2016, we were once again invited to join Beth and her team for a spiritual retreat with a difference, entitled Pathways to Transformation. We had not planned to attend the Geneva conference this year and apparently it had not been on Beth's agenda either, but a sudden inspiration had led to a more intimate style of retreat, focusing on the inner person and allowing time for personal creativity and expression. It really worked. The energy was great, the small group of some forty people gelled perfectly, the sun shone throughout and the chateau with its immaculate gardens and grounds provided the perfect context for spiritual contemplation and retreat. Quiet moments of meditation in the chapel contrasted with the buzz of conversation at dinner and the energy of movement, mantra and dance.

One of the highlights for me was a simple, guided walking meditation late one sunny afternoon. We walked in silence to a slow, gentle rhythm. I became aware of the different textures beneath my feet: the grate of the gravel, the crunch of the stones, the softly giving sand and grass and the refreshing stillness. I saw more clearly the breathtaking beauty and expanse of the immediate landscape and distant snow-capped mountains, the occasional sailing boat white-trimmed against the horizon, the sunshine radiating from the surface of the water, the perfect smoothness of newly-mown lawns and carefully tended farmers' fields and the occasional flower popping up through the dense forest of wild undergrowth. There was absolute joy in softly moving to the gentle pace of a walking meditation and for a beautiful moment I felt the thrill of just 'being'. Walking would never feel quite the same again.

Pilgrimage

Linda and I had derived great pleasure and satisfaction from organising and hosting New Thought events and conferences. They helped and healed a lot of people along the way as well as satisfying our own need for creative spiritual expression. But conferences require a tremendous amount of planning and preparation, as well as a substantial commitment of time, energy and resources, and we found ourselves resisting the call for a third UK Abundant Living conference.

On the other hand, the concept of one-day, one-speaker seminars began to grow in appeal. We had already located a highly suitable local venue with excellent acoustics, seating and parking for a hundred people, a top rate sound system with an enthusiastic sound engineer. All we needed was a top rate speaker…

So we treated, let go… and then came the `phone call.

It was Cynthia James, an ebullient associate minister from the Mile Hi Center for Spiritual Living in Denver, Colorado, the home of Dr Roger Teel. Cynthia had heard about us from Dr Roger. She was planning a trip to Ireland and wondered if we would be interested in hosting a workshop for her in the UK as she had published a new book entitled *What Will Set You Free*, all about healing through forgiveness. Passionate about teaching people how to lead purposeful and powerful lives, Cynthia simply exuded enthusiasm. Divine synchronicity. We had our first speaker. She was a pleasure to work with and stunned the audience with her sheer overflowing exuberance and colourful presence.

"I love being alive," she said. "I am excited every day to get up and see what incredible gifts await me. Many people label me as 'enthusiastic' because I am committed to living each moment full out. I totally feel inspired and motivated to be all that I came here to be."

The following year, we received a `phone call from the personal assistant to David Ault, the senior minister at the Atlanta Center for Spiritual Living in Georgia, USA. Apparently, David was planning a trip to London with his partner and "would love to do a workshop" for us, having heard about us from his friend, Karen Drucker. He had also published a new book, called *The Grass is Greener Here*. David was a very charismatic speaker with an irresistible charm that made him an instant hit with our UK audience. Indeed, when Beth Linguri enquired whether we could recommend any speakers for the Geneva Conference, he was top of the list.

"Universal law," says David, "faithfully delivers to my doorstep of experience everything I habitually adopt as my belief – not because my beliefs are any more accurate than another's but because the law is an impersonal one, bringing to manifestation the sum total of our focus.

"It was Buddha who taught, 'The mind is everything. What you think, you become.' If I choose to think I am capable and worthy more so than not, this impersonal spiritual law corresponds to my choice and offers a world that reflects back to me."

These seminar days would begin with live music followed by a brief introductory talk. After a short break there would be a question and answer session, and after lunch an afternoon session devoted to an interactive workshop. The day would end with a prayer and a blessing and a few final words from our visiting speaker. The events were proving popular and we were building a strong and loyal following. So when, in the spring of 2014, we announced the visit of California-based spiritual teacher, author and TV presenter, Dr Harry Morgan Moses, we received a flood of enquiries and advance registrations.

Dr Harry was senior minister of the Spirit Works Center for Spiritual Living in Burbank, California, and was actually a bit of a New Thought celebrity, having featured in the films *Living Luminaries* and *What is New Thought?* He also hosted his own TV show, *The Moses Show*, and was the author of several bestselling books. But what we loved most about him was his relaxed, easy-going, Californian charm and accessible style of presentation.

His seminar, The Heaven Experience, proved to be one of the most popular and successful that we had run and when the day was over people just did not want to leave.

"We could have carried on all night," commented one participant. Dr Harry was so interesting and stimulating that, as the day unfolded, the audience became ever more engaged, especially when he recounted the remarkable story of his own 'miracle healing' and how the power of Spirit had changed his life. There is nothing like a personal testimonial to galvanise interest and this one had all the ingredients of a Hollywood movie. His message: always know that there is a Power for Good in the universe, greater than us, that we can use.

"Happiness is an inside job," says Dr Harry, "and it's not so much what happens, as how we perceive or interpret the event.

"Salvation is freedom, freedom to live your life in purpose is your right by divine inheritance. Claim the kingdom, live your life fulfilled and share your love with everyone who touches the arena of your experience. Indeed, live the cosmic adventure. Look for the good wherever it is and add to it."

Happiness is an inside job.

Dr Kathy Hearn

David and Linda Serlin

We have met and worked with many wise and inspiring spiritual teachers during the various stages and chapters of our own spiritual journey. From our visits to Stansted Hall to discovering the Bournemouth Science of Mind church, from Asilomar to our two landmark UK conferences and our visits to Switzerland, these and other unique and remarkable experiences have opened our eyes to the reality of Spirit and the power of creative thought.

One of our earliest spiritual mentors had been Gordon Higginson, a remarkable medium and a wise and spiritual man. He had advised going on a spiritual pilgrimage every now and again to refresh the soul and to reconnect with Source. For a while, our trips to Asilomar had fitted the bill perfectly but in 2014 we embarked on another, rather different sort of pilgrimage.

Two hours north of Brazil's capital, Brasilia, travelling through vast expanses of open terrain, cattle rearing country and past innumerable 'cantinas', you will come to Abadiânia, a tiny village set off the main highway and dominated by the Casa de Dom Inácio de Loyola. This is the base of Brazilian healer João Teixeira de Faria, known as João de Deus, or John of God. We had read much and heard more about him and were finally inspired to action by an article in the Science of Mind magazine by Dr Roger Teel, who had visited Abadiânia himself and clearly had been impressed by what he had experienced at the Casa. Some intuitive urge seemed to suggest it was the right time for us to make this particular pilgrimage too.

After weeks of careful planning, we headed for the airport to catch the early morning flight to Lisbon and from there the long-haul to Brasilia, leaving London at dawn and arriving in Brazil late afternoon local time to blazing heat with temperatures in the high twenties and a warm, friendly welcome. We were to spend the weekend in Brasilia to meet up with the rest of our tour before embarking on the journey north. We checked in to the Naoum Plaza Hotel to be confronted with the fact that nobody spoke a word of English, so we had to resort to facial expressions and hand gestures to indicate our needs. The smiling receptionist eventually understood and found us a room with a view.

We spent the rest of the weekend sunbathing by the pool and exploring the locality before joining the rest of the tour on the Sunday evening for an introductory dinner. The typically Brazilian food was amazing and the bevy of characters who had congregated for this particular tour were equally interesting and gregarious. From all ages and backgrounds, from all over the world, people had come together, drawn by the fascination of healing, legendary miracles and the wonder of connecting with some deeper spiritual purpose. Some, quiet and reserved, were preoccupied with the journey ahead. Others, animated and exuberant, shared veteran stories from previous visits and told tales of amazing miracles that either they or someone close to them had experienced. And others, perhaps like us, came out of curiosity, wanting to find out more and experience the intrigue of this Mecca of healing. We soon struck up new friendships and connections with our fellow travellers and with our congenial and very knowledgeable tour leader, Heather, who was to guide us adeptly all the way to Abadiânia, hundreds of miles north and a million light years away from the hustle and bustle of Brasilia.

Brazil was very much a young country, albeit with deep traditions dating back into the long distant past, still finding its feet in the modern world. The clash of cultures was no more evident than on this long journey north as the built-up skyscrapers gave way to tiny villages, wide open panoramic landscapes and vistas more akin to a Wild West movie. As we stopped for a drink at a roadside cantina, we could almost imagine John Wayne riding up on his trusted steed, a cloud of dust behind him, wiping the grimy sweat from his forehead as he raised his Stetson before slowly dismounting and swinging open the doors to the bar. This was real cowboy country, where the slow march of modernisation had not yet made its mark.

Before we knew it, the conversation during the trip having been so invigorating that time had flown, we arrived at Abadiânia and our 'poussada' (hotel) for the week. The sun was still full on, with temperatures well into the eighties, and what struck us most at first was the peace and quiet, even though the main highway was minutes away. Surrounded by palm trees and carefully tended gardens, our little hotel offered a friendly welcome, the coolness of the interior a pleasant relief after the hot and dusty journey.

The village was crisscrossed by small, quiet roads lined with poussadas and small shops and artisan boutiques selling memorabilia, books, crystals, artefacts and all sorts of accessories for the thousands of pilgrims who descend on this sleepy hamlet all year round. There was a curious blend of the New Age and ancient traditions and superstitions, and despite the inevitable commercialism there was something quite appealing and attractive about the whole atmosphere. A feature on *The Oprah Winfrey Show* had dramatically raised the profile of the place and had broadcast its message to millions around the world, bringing a relative affluence to the area, which seemed to be flourishing under the benevolent patronage of the Casa.

Back at our poussada, appropriately named the Hotel Rei Davi (King David Hotel), our little tribe of about twenty gathered together for an ample and delicious evening meal, lovingly prepared by our guide, Heather. The caring and compassionate atmosphere was noticeable, as was Heather's obvious dedication to John of God and the work of the Casa. As the sun began to set and with the air still pleasantly warm, we were invited to walk to the Casa about ten minutes away for a taste of things to come.

We walked in respectful silence along the now deserted streets, with just the sound of the cicadas in the background and an underlying hum of excited anticipation, feeling the energy of what lay ahead. But the Casa itself was not quite as we had imagined (perhaps a Spanish villa with wild, rambling gardens). Set in its own grounds and surrounded by a low brick wall and tall gates, with the obligatory parking area for coaches, it comprised an extensive complex of low-rise buildings clad in blue and white, with a ribbon of covered verandas and walkways to protect visitors from the midday sun. At the heart of the complex were beautifully landscaped gardens and lawns, with carved benches and shaded paths and a variety of exotic trees and shrubs. Perched up high, with breathtaking views over the surrounding countryside, was a simple meditation area.

At the very heart of the complex were the healing rooms: the Great Hall, which accommodated hundreds of visiting pilgrims and patients each day, the Current Rooms, the Energy Centre and the Surgery Rooms, in which the various forms of healing took place. We could just peer through the windows of the Great Hall to see portraits of the various spirit guides, doctors and 'Entities' (as they were called), who purportedly worked with and through the entranced John of God, adorning the walls. It was all beautifully laid out, well organised, orderly and spotlessly clean. Now deserted, in the silence and stillness with just a gentle breeze blowing, we could sense the special atmosphere, the echoes of past healings and miracles shrouded in mystery.

The following day was a rest day so we relaxed in the gardens and wandered through the side streets of Abadiânia, browsing the shops, sampling the wares, buying souvenirs and feeling the mood and laid-back atmosphere of this amazing place. During the afternoon and well into the evening, Heather filled us in with the intriguing history and background to the Casa as well as sharing many remarkable stories and testimonials to healing through John of God, including her own. The gleam in her eye and the enthusiasm with which she spoke were clear evidence of her commitment and devotion to the work of the Casa.

As the stars twinkled high in the night sky, Heather described our programme for the next day and forewarned us about the mysterious 'orbs', balls of light energy that appear randomly all around the area. Indeed, a photograph I took at night through the window of the hotel revealed an array of peculiar ball-shaped lights... Who knows? After all, this was a place of spiritual energy and anything might happen.

Next day we were now invited actually to participate in the activity of the Casa. There were strict ground rules and protocols to be observed. We were to assemble outside the hotel and, with Heather as our guide, walk silently and respectfully to the Casa. Part of the ritual was that everyone dressed in white, apparently to make our auras more visible to the spirit Entities who worked with John of God. It was a somewhat surreal sight to see hundreds of people all dressed in white descending on the Casa from all directions, like something out of a sci-fi movie.

We were directed to the Great Hall and as we shuffled along the sheltered walkways – it was still early but already the heat was beginning to build – we could barely withhold our excitement. At last we were to experience John of God in action... But as we entered the Hall, with hundreds of people already seated, we soon realised that patience and forbearance would be needed. It was going to be a long, hot wait.

Being part of Heather's group, she being considered a prestigious 'daughter of the Casa', we were directed right to the front of the Hall beside the raised platform onto which John of God and his helpers would eventually appear and perform psychic surgery. We might have been at the front where the action was and with a clear view of proceedings, but it also meant standing up for the whole duration, two or three hours. And far from being quiet and serene, there was a constant chatter from the assembled crowd – some seated comfortably, others standing, anxiously awaiting their turn for healing or 'an audience with the Entities'.

There were people in wheelchairs and on stretchers, some having travelled long distances to be there. There were local people, well versed in the routine and familiar with the pattern of events, hugging, kissing and shaking hands with old friends. There were those on a sacred pilgrimage and those for whom this was now a regular event.

In true laid-back South American style, it soon became clear that no-one was in any sort of hurry. After a couple of hours, a well-presented man in a grey suit stepped onto the platform and addressed the audience in fluent Portuguese. His words were met by ripples of laughter so we could only assume that he was either well known by the audience or was a sort of warm-up act for the main presentation. When he had finished, another person took to the stage and continued the dialogue, though now with somewhat more dignity and aplomb. We could hardly understand a word that was being spoken. All of this was a little frustrating but we realised that this was a very different culture, with different traditions and beliefs, so we would just have to put aside any expectations, judgments and preconceptions and go with the flow.

After a couple of hours patiently waiting – and by now we had got used to the constant whirr and whine of the electric ceiling fans – we became blended into the energy and atmosphere of the packed hall, no longer observers but participants in this extraordinary healing ritual. We moved and swayed with the throng, carried along on the crest of a wave of expectation. Then a hush descended on the room, a door opened and John of God stepped onto the platform accompanied by a bevy of white-coated assistants. It was a serious and serene moment, save for a couple of knowing gestures to familiar members of the audience.

A volunteer from the audience was invited to experience psychic surgery. The assistants handed John of God a series of instruments such as scalpels and knives, and he made some short, sharp and apparently painless incisions in the skin of the patient, who expressed no pain but just stepped back and fell into the arms of a waiting helper. The wound area was quickly dabbed and sealed and the patient, apparently happy and content, was escorted to another room for recuperation.

It was a curious procedure to say the least and we couldn't help wondering what the volunteer's actual problem was and how they were responding. Was this simply to demonstrate the power of the phenomenon that is psychic surgery? Whatever, it all added to the air of mystery. After about fifteen minutes it was all over and John of God returned to the anteroom to prepare himself for the next stage of the healing process, an audience with the Entities.

Together with a hundred or so others, we were invited to join a queue in the centre of the Great Hall for an audience with the now entranced John of God or, more specifically, with whichever Entity was in attendance that day. The spirit team comprised a host of interesting and colourful characters, apparently, with some who had lived on Earth hundreds of years ago and made notable contributions to humanity in the fields of science, medicine, politics and spirituality. These included Augusto de Almeida Monjardino, Dom Inácio de Loyola himself, who had lived on the site of the Casa and after whom it had been named, and Francisco Cândido ('Chico') Xavier, a highly esteemed author, humanitarian and Spiritist medium who had only relatively recently passed on.

Eventually our lengthy queue filed its way slowly and silently into what was called the Current Room, past rows of people seated in silent meditation (or in some cases fast asleep). We were met by some kind of powerful electric energy that drew us in as we shuffled slowly towards the raised dais on which sat John of God, now entranced and controlled by one of the Entities.

It was a surreal moment as Heather briefly introduced us to the Entity, who nodded in acknowledgment, scribbled a few pencil notes on a piece of paper, handed it to Heather and then bade us goodbye. The whole encounter lasted only a few seconds. According to the paper, I had been designated to have healing surgery the following day, while a slightly disappointed Linda was prescribed a series of 'crystal baths', to take some herbs and to meditate.

Somewhat bemused, we staggered out into the bright afternoon sunlight, found a shaded spot in the beautiful gardens, and reviewed the events of the day. There were dozens of other people milling around all at varying stages of the healing process. This was not healing as we were accustomed to back home in the UK, involving instead a lot of ritual and esoteric superstition that paid homage to local customs, culture and religious traditions. It was not quite what we had expected – but by now we had learned to expect the unexpected.

Back at our hotel we enjoyed a late lunch with our fellow travellers, swapping stories of the day's events, before Heather announced that we had been invited to sit in the Current Room at the Casa that afternoon. This was a privilege but one that, as we were soon to discover, would require a great deal of patience and self-discipline. What we had let ourselves in for now?

Linda and I had been accustomed to 'sitting in the power' in meditation, tuning in to Spirit at Stansted for maybe thirty to forty-five minutes at a time. But here we were expected to sit silently and still on hard, unforgiving wooden benches for two to three hours without moving. It seemed an almost impossible task, yet within minutes we had sunk into a deep, relaxed, almost hypnotic state with just the sound of a helper's voice in the background reciting poems and prayers in a variety of languages. After a while we had lost all track of time, the background voices disappearing into a distant, dreamlike haze and it was only the creeping numbness in our backs and buttocks that brought us back to consciousness. A bell sounded to mark the end of the session and together with several dozen other meditators we crept quietly through the Current Rooms, careful not to disturb the mediums who sat in silent vigil close to the entranced Entity.

The following day I was to return and be at the receiving end of that energy. Dining at the hotel was a jovial affair as we sat around a long table in the garden, sharing stories of our experiences at the Casa. That night we both slept soundly, still feeling the benefit and after-effects of that lengthy meditation.

The next day dawned bright and we were up early, feeling a mixture of excitement and apprehension. Heather had forewarned me that after the healing surgery I might feel rather tired and groggy and would need to come back to the hotel to rest. While Linda left to have her crystal baths, I joined the audience in the Great Hall, waited patiently through the now familiar introductory talks and then lined up with the other hundred or so people earmarked for healing that day.

After a short while the door to the surgery room was opened, and a white-coated assistant beckoned us enter and take a seat along the multiple rows of wooden benches. It was a tight squeeze with little room to spare, and the proximity to so many people and the warmth of the air contributed to a heavy, almost oppressive atmosphere. I could barely keep my eyes open – or was it the build-up of spirit energy in the room?

We were instructed to place one hand over our heart and direct the healing by our thoughts to where it was most needed. There were no physical healers present, although apparently a host of spirit Entities were wandering amongst us, performing whatever healing intercessions were deemed necessary. The whole process lasted about ten minutes, following which we were ushered into a small anteroom to be debriefed. Patients needing personal attention or assistance were attended to, a prayer and a blessing were read in Portuguese and then we were released into the afternoon sunshine. Heather's earlier advice came to mind as suddenly I was feeling extremely tired, rather disorientated, and I welcomed the sight of a local taxi that had thoughtfully been pre-booked to take us back to the hotel.

Following healing surgery we were supposed to rest for twenty-four hours, take our meals in silence and retire to our rooms to sleep as much as possible. Everyone at the hotel was familiar with the routine and respected the silence and solitude of those who had received healing. What was strange was that I did not want to talk, I did not want company or any distraction but was pleased just to rest in my room and listen to music. I must have slept for hours and had some strange, particularly vivid dreams.

When I awoke later that evening, I slipped downstairs to dine alone. By morning my lethargy had completely lifted to be replaced by a quiet, subdued feeling. I was relieved, however, when the twenty-four hours were up and I was able to return to normality.

Linda, on the other hand, reacted very differently to healing at the Casa. Having enjoyed a series of very pleasant and relaxing crystal baths, she was a little frustrated that there might not be an opportunity for her to experience healing before we were due to leave. Heather kindly managed, however, to arrange a healing surgery session for her. Far from being groggy like me, Linda came back tingling with energy, buzzing with electricity and full of vitality. It took her a while to calm down and settle back into normality, although the after-effects lingered for several days.

It had been a whirlwind of a week, something totally different. In a world of its own, Abadiânia revolved completely around the Casa and we had been drawn inextricably into the charm and magic of this extraordinary place. When it was time to say goodbye, it was like bidding farewell to old friends; over those few days in Brazil, we had grown close to our little group and we hoped that they would all find what they were looking for.

On the long flight home we reviewed our stay and our experience of John of God. While we personally had not experienced any healing miracles, we realised that the very existence of such a place as the Casa – a haven of peace and healing, attracting thousands of people from all over the world and offering hope, solace and renewed purpose to so many – was very special and we felt blessed to have shared in its unique energy on our own spiritual pilgrimage.

We also reviewed the peculiar rituals and protocols we were supposed to adhere to following our healing surgery. For the next forty-five days we were to abstain from alcohol (easy), spicy foods such as chilli and hot peppers (no problem), vigorous exercise and activities (difficult), prolonged use of computers and electronic equipment (feasible) and sex (impossible). It was a rigid routine and, coupled with regular intake of 'specially blessed' herbs, proved quite a challenge. Still, we

Where Two or More Are Gathered

We were sitting right at the back of the room, ready for a quick exit when the lecture was finished. A friend was running a course at Stansted; this was the final session of the afternoon and the popular medium was addressing a packed room with nearly a hundred people present when she stopped short mid-sentence.

"I don't usually do this,' she confessed, "in fact, it's quite rare. But I have an urgent message for someone here." She scanned the audience and her gaze rested on us. "It's for you," she said, surprised. "But why is it so urgent?" We explained that we were only there for the day and were shortly about to leave.

There were two messages, one from Linda's Dad who had passed several years before; it was particularly pertinent and reassuring, and even the medium sensed the emotional urgency behind it. The other was an intriguing communication from an unnamed source.

"We are aware of the times you both sit together in the silence for Spirit. And we want to let you know that where two or more are gathered, we are there." We were surprised to realise that even in our quiet moments when we pray, or even just discuss spiritual matters, we are in the power and presence of Spirit.

"We recognise you by your light," the message continued, "and when you gather together with like minds, that light shines even brighter."

This was a gratifying reference to the spiritual work we were doing. It had been after a fantastic trip to Asilomar in 1999 that we had been inspired to start our own study group. At first, we had no idea how, where or when it would work but were eager to make a firm commitment to share the teaching that was serving us so well. Little did we realise at the time that it would become such an integral part of our lives. No sooner had the idea seeded itself in our consciousness than we happened to meet a delightful American couple who were planning to relocate to London for their work. They were keen to stay connected to Science of Mind and when they heard about our fledgling study group they wanted to get involved. We had our first members!

Our little group grew quickly, attracting new members along the way, and those early days were fun and exciting. We were treading new ground and our early forays into the world of metaphysics bore some unexpected dividends. This was before anyone had even heard of the law of attraction and years before *The Secret* was published.

We read avidly and accrued an impressive library of New Thought classics, from Raymond Barker, Joseph Murphy and Catherine Ponder to Florence Schinn and of course Ernest Holmes. We studied affirmative prayer and spiritual mind treatment, and put the principles into practice as best we knew how. Within a year or two, we were rewarded with concrete confirmation in our personal lives of the efficacy of treatment. We learned by experience how to 'let go and let God' before there were any outward signs of success and despite all appearances to the contrary. We were tried and tested and went through a tough apprenticeship before we finally earned our stripes and qualified as Science of Mind practitioners. It was a journey of faith that gave us a new and deeper understanding of the nature of God and of Spirit.

In the early days of our study group we used to meet on a Sunday afternoon, alternating venues in different people's houses, improvising and experimenting, gradually creating our own style and identity until suddenly it all came together. As we delved deeper into the teachings, we put our own particular brand on things and moved from borrowed ideas to expressing our own individual insights and interpretations.

As more and more people came to hear about the group our numbers steadily increased so we moved the meetings to the comfort of our own home. Rows of seats were set out on a Sunday evening and our guests offered food for thought, nourishment for the soul, and apple juice and biscuits (handed out eagerly by our son, who would often stay up late to say the welcome blessing before he went to bed).

Following our two conferences there was a surge of interest and an influx of new members. It soon became clear that we would need larger premises to accommodate the ever-increasing numbers. By chance we happened to hear about The Meeting Room, a beautiful, private, peaceful space located just a few minutes from where we lived. Overlooking a pretty country garden and used exclusively for healing, meditation and alternative therapies, it exuded the perfect spiritual atmosphere and seemed ideal for our needs. The Meeting Room has served us well over the years and after a typical Sunday session, as the candles are extinguished and the lights dimmed, there remains a special feeling summed up in the words of a prayer, "Surely the presence of God is in this place."

Today, the study group continues to thrive, shining an even brighter light out into the world. The Kings Langley New Thought/ Spiritual Living Group, born from modest beginnings all those years ago, is now the longest running Science of Mind group in the UK. It has gone through many incarnations, attracting people from all ages, backgrounds, beliefs and walks of life, and reflects the unique energy and character of the people involved. Some people come tentatively to test the water, wondering what New Thought is all about, only to discover how modern, relevant and practical it really is. Others may come with a particular burning issue or challenge, and find the solution they are seeking though affirmative prayer. And many come simply to experience the magic and mystery of spiritual connection and community.

Every meeting is unique. There will be inspirational readings and uplifting music, spontaneous discussion and lively debate, insightful comments and lots of laughter. In a typical two and a half hour session we may cover a wide range of subject matter, all based on spiritual principles. One day the theme may be 'gratitude and forgiveness', on another 'prosperity and abundance' or 'the power of I am'. Underlying all the readings, meditations, affirmations and processes is the intention to apply the principles, to make metaphysics relevant and resonant with our everyday hopes, needs and challenges.

We always begin our meetings, which often resemble a family reunion, with music, a candlelit blessing and an inspirational reading. Our time together is sacred and we bless the meeting, acknowledging the power and presence of Spirit. The agenda weaves through a magical pattern including affirmations and treatments by Ernest Holmes, Louise Hay or Florence Scovel Schinn. We select suitable readings to uplift and inspire – one member called us the Spiritual Upliftment Group – and music to blend with the subject and shift the energy to an even higher level. We practise fun processes to lighten the load, perhaps focusing on a particular book, a classic from the past or a more modern version, to stimulate discussion. And we take time to share, to listen to often amazing testimonials from people who have experienced the principles in practice. This is what we are all about – practical spirituality.

We might have got our spiritual 'fix' from conferences, seminars and weekend retreats, coming home on a high, cocooned in a bubble we hoped wouldn't burst. But unless we anchor those feelings they may soon dissolve and dissipate. It is through our regular meetings, however, that we find continuity and connection, a refuge and safe haven to recharge our spiritual batteries and rekindle our passion, purpose and motivation.

Napoleon Hill, author of *Think and Grow Rich*, proposed the idea of 'a mastermind alliance', a group of spiritually like-minded people who come together to pool their resources of wisdom, expertise and experience in support of a common purpose for the highest good of all. He also advised us only to share our hopes and dreams with those people who understand, sympathise and support us in our endeavours. For many people, our study group represents such a spiritual oasis, a reminder that we are never alone, that dreams do come true and miracles can happen. And little miracles do happen all the time: health conditions turn around, new relationships are forged, career opportunities are transformed or work situations improved, lost items are suddenly found... unexpected good arising 'from nowhere to now here'!

> *'It's really great to be with such loving and caring people,'* wrote one member, *"sharing happiness instead of doom and gloom. I have been working on my affirmations and found they have helped me get through things in a happy way.'*

> *'Thank you for a wonderful evening,'* wrote another, *"it put everything into place and there were lots of good comments and reinforcement of the power of positive thought and the law of attraction. I thoroughly enjoyed it.'*

> *'Last Sunday's gathering has to have been the most uplifting to date. Everyone who attended was just so positive and engaging. I found the whole evening a truly wonderful and enriching experience.'*

Organising, running and hosting our group has been a privilege and a pleasure for Linda and me. Our Sunday evening meetings have become an integral part of our spiritual practice, and we plan and prepare our agenda carefully, often with a topical theme in mind. And then divine synchronicity takes over. Some people may come with a specific question or concern, only to find their answer tucked within a reading or affirmation that may seem to have been specially designed just for them.

For Carol, a dear friend of ours, coming to our conferences, discovering Science of Mind and attending our study group and seminars has been the catalyst for a string of miracles in her life. Carol is now living her dream, but it was not always that way. She was a senior nursing manager with a healthy income and was happily married, but she was under a lot of stress that was beginning to take its toll.

"I had struggled through another difficult day," she explains. "I was bone tired, upset and stressed to the limit. I realised something had to give when I got the 'phone call from David. 'Have you heard of Science of Mind?' he asked, 'and a book called *The Secret*?' I hadn't, and with the mood I was in I didn't want to either!

"My husband Colin and I had met David and Lin a number of years earlier on a course at Stansted Hall. I recognised them both to be honest, open-minded people, so I took a deep breath and explained that I was under a lot of pressure at work and I just couldn't get my head round anything else at the time. But David continued, 'Look, get yourself a copy of *The Secret* and read it. I'm sure it will help. By the way, Lin and I are planning a conference in Kings Langley and we'd love you both to come.'

"I trusted David's judgment and got a copy of the book. In my usual rushed way – I was used to reading emails and work papers quickly – I crashed through it and frankly could not find any meaning in it. David called to see if we were going to book for the conference and I said 'No'. It was just too much what with all the packing and ongoing demands from my work. I felt overwhelmed but my husband Colin, and another chat with Lin, eventually persuaded me to book.

"I was sceptical and didn't know what to expect as we embarked on the four-hour journey from Newcastle, where we lived, to Hertfordshire. When we arrived at the Rudolf Steiner School I was taken aback. It was packed. There was music and laughter. I couldn't believe it and I thought to myself, what on Earth am I doing here? What am I going to learn here? I had read a bit about Science of Mind but I said to David, 'If this is a bit like the Moonies or some sort of cult, I am going straight back home.' He laughed and just said, 'Wait and see.'

"As the conference began, I remember thinking, 'I know all this stuff. I've always known it.' Looking back, I cannot even recall the moment I felt the change begin, but the speakers spoke with such passion and emotion I remember feeling something I hadn't felt for ages, and that was joy. Joy was the missing piece from my life. I suddenly felt filled with energy and happiness. And happiness, as one of the speakers said, is an inside job.

"There was talk of affirmative prayer and spiritual mind treatment and of a God who loves everybody regardless of their faith or background. But what struck me most was the positivity in the words and music. I heard how we are all connected to the one divine spirit and that if we change our story, we can change our lives. The speakers spoke about thriving and not just surviving and this story was beginning to hit home. It was the most magical time.

"I filled a journal full of affirmations that weekend. I learned that if I worked on the inner me then the outward transformation would take place. I affirmed that life was good, that I wanted to go from stressed to blessed, from unhealthy to healthy, from angry to happy. I wrote that the power to manifest was readily available to me and everyone else. I read other authors on the subject, including Florence Schinn, and I began to do mind treatments. I was hooked.

"I had begun a journey of inward transformation that weekend. I had arrived at that first seminar in true pain. I didn't know that I would find the key to unlock my turmoil and transport me to a better version of me.

"I continued doing my affirmations and changes continued to happen. Every now and again I might have a little wobble. I would get frightened and upset, the old me still hanging on to what did not serve me, and then David and Lin would send me marvellous mind treatments, which I still have. It was not always easy to get out of my own way, to let go of control of the so-called status that my job gave me. My initial introduction to Science of Mind, however, changed me in so many ways. As my life changed, I developed a deep knowing that the universe would support me in all that I do.

"I now live in a constant stream of gratitude for all that I have. I take pleasure in simple things. My whole outlook has changed. I choose to be happy, to feel joy every day. It isn't all pixies and unicorns, it's life in its fullest form, constantly evolving. I no longer feel stuck. Science of Mind has saved my sanity in so many ways and, even when I let go of the steering wheel, Spirit directs me to where I need to be.

"I cannot begin to think what my life would have been like had I said 'No' to that first gathering in Kings Langley. I thank the universe for Lin and David, for not giving up on the stubborn woman that I am and for opening up a whole new world for me. I have since attended a lot of David's and Lin's study groups and seminars and, although we may live hundreds of miles apart, Science of Mind has been the glue that cements the friendship we have shared. I am so grateful. And so it is."

It was one of those gloriously sunny, crisp winter mornings, with a vivid blue sky and not a cloud in sight. We were down in Bournemouth celebrating Christmas with our family at the Durley Hall Hotel situated on Bournemouth's West Cliff. Wrapped up warm, we headed for the seafront bracing ourselves against the chilly breeze that blew in from the ocean. But with the sun full on it felt more like a spring day.

"Wouldn't it be great to spend a weekend here later in the year?" suggested Linda. "I could just visualise us relaxing by the pool with a cool drink and a good book."

It had been a fun few days and on Boxing Day afternoon the lively and enterprising entertainments team, led by a charming lady called Lisa, planned a Countdown competition. We joined forces with our friend Sue and sat down together to pit our wits against the finest the Durley Hall could muster. Round by round, the competition became keener as one team after another bowed out until finally there was just us and one other defiant family who refused to surrender.

The final round was a tie-breaker and we had to nominate one member of our team to stand against the opposition. Linda quickly volunteered, being a master of crosswords and Sudoku and relishing the challenge. One by one the scrambled letters appeared on the screen, a jumble of apparent gobbledegook. The tension was mounting, timing was crucial. The opposition looked puzzled but Linda had a look of victory on her face. Even before all the letters had been completed and organised, she knew what the answer was.

"Pumpernickel!" she shouted gleefully. How on Earth had she deciphered that word from the random selection in front of her? But she was right and we had won.

With a smile and a hug, Lisa handed Linda an envelope containing the mystery prize. Winners of the various other competitions that afternoon had been rewarded with bottles of champagne, boxes of chocolate and vouchers for a free aromatherapy massage in the hotel spa. But when Linda opened the envelope, she let out a shriek of excitement: we had won a free weekend for two at the Durley Hall Hotel and Spa.

"My goodness," I thought. "That's just what Linda had wished for. Now that's what we call manifesting."

While writing the final draft for my first book, we spent some time in Mallorca in a small studio apartment overlooking the sea in Cala Mayor near Palma. Ideas flowed freely, although the constant tapping on my typewriter proved a constant source of irritation to our less than tolerant next door neighbours. Moments of inspiration were interspersed with occasional meanderings along the beach enjoying the view and lapping up the warm sunshine. We promised ourselves that when the job was done we would come back to enjoy a few days of pure sun, sea and relaxation.

Well, that was the plan but, when we arrived back in Mallorca the following April for a week's spring break, the weather gods clearly had other ideas. The sun did not shine. In fact it rained the whole time, that dull, grey, incessant, demoralising rain from dawn to dusk that wears you down and seeps into your clothes and hair. Somehow we managed to keep our spirits up and spent our time playing music, singing songs, walking and talking and to some extent laughing it off. We were quite relieved, however, when it was time to leave and the taxi arrived to take us back to Palma.

On the way to the airport, the rain suddenly stopped, the sun broke through the clouds and the sky turned from a dirty grey to a lustrous, dazzling blue. For the first time that week we felt the luxuriant warmth of real Mediterranean sunshine.

"Typical," said Linda, "we're going home and the weather changes. I wish we could stay just one more day and enjoy the sunshine."

Well… When we arrived at Palma Airport it seemed unusually quiet. We were early so we took a leisurely stroll around, browsing the airport shops, before checking in. Strangely enough, we couldn't see any signs telling us where our check-in desk was and on enquiring at the Information Desk we were met by blank stares and quizzical looks. We were beginning to feel a little uneasy…

A well-spoken attendant politely advised us that we were in the right terminal building but our flight had already departed hours before and without us.

Once we got over the initial shock at having missed the flight, we quickly inspected our tickets and itinerary and realised what had happened. It was the beginning of April and the time when flight schedules changed from 'winter' to 'summer', a fact our travel agent had obviously overlooked. Whereas our tickets (which we had not looked at) were correct, our itinerary (which we had looked at) was incorrect.

We could have been angry with the travel agent, but that would not have helped the situation. We could have been angry with ourselves or each other, but that would not have helped either. We realised that anger and blame were pointless. We just had to take responsibility for the situation we had found ourselves in and make the most of it.

Then, all of a sudden, our concerns vanished and an amazing sense of calm came over us. It was a beautiful day with the first sun we had seen all week, so we were going to make the most of it. We 'phoned home and rebooked our flights for the next day, then took a taxi back into Palma where we booked into a hotel overlooking the harbour. The early afternoon sun evaporated any lingering damp on the walkways and we enjoyed a wonderful bonus day strolling along the seafront, admiring the gleaming white yachts and sailing boats in the harbour, relaxing in the sun and getting a welcome bit of tan to take home with us. That evening we enjoyed a superb meal at a local fish restaurant before returning to our comfortable hotel suite having had the best day of the holiday. Extra expense, yes, but worth every penny. When we arrived home, we felt relaxed and realised that the last bonus day had changed the whole mood of our holiday.

It's not so much what happens as how we may perceive and interpret the event. The ever-listening universe had picked up on our thoughts, acknowledged our silent wish and turned a small disaster into a happy ending.

A Golden Thread

Looking back at our journey so far, we can discern a definite pattern, a golden thread of divine synchronicity weaving through the tapestry of our lives. It has manifested in the many invitations and opportunities that have come our way and to which, fortunately, we said 'Yes', even though they might have stretched our boundaries and propelled us out of our comfort zone into a whole new world of possibilities.

"Change is inevitable," says Dr Harry Morgan Moses, "but growth is optional."

From our first fortuitous visit to the Arthur Findlay College and meeting Gordon Higginson, to our discovery of New Thought, Science of Mind and Asilomar, growth was in the stars.

Dr Ernest Holmes said, "We were born to be happy, to be abundantly supplied with every good thing, to have fun in living, to consciously unite with the divine power that is around us and within us and to grow and expand forever."

There have been difficult and challenging times too, and this is true for all of us. But whatever we have experienced has only contributed to who and what we are now. When we stand back and see the bigger picture, we can recognise that there is a divine purpose behind all things; then life takes on new meaning and, out of our doubts and disappointments, hidden blessings may emerge. And having someone special to share the journey with us is a gift to be cherished.

Several years ago, there was a clever television advertisement showing a man holding a briefcase while walking along a busy street. Suddenly a stranger looms out of nowhere, grabs the briefcase and pushes the man to the ground. Our immediate instinct is to make a judgment, based on the evidence at hand, that a crime has been committed. But then, as we are shown the bigger picture, a different story emerges. A large object is about to fall dangerously from the roof of a nearby building and would have struck the man had the stranger not intervened and actually saved his life. By changing our perspective and thus our interpretation of the event, the villain becomes the hero.

Seeing the bigger picture, looking at life from different angles and a wider viewpoint, is what New Thought is all about. It is so easy to make immediate judgments, based on our preconceptions of life, and to take on board limiting attitudes and beliefs. In particular, New Thought reminds us that while we may grow up assuming that life happens to us, that we are powerless victims of circumstance, the truth is that we are active participants in the dance, co-creators in the game of life.

From my understanding, we are not merely observers but actively involved in the expansion of the universe, the behaviour of cells and atoms and in the way our lives unfold by the nature of our thoughts, beliefs and expectations. A quiet revolution is taking place and we are only just beginning to realise the immense implications and potential of the Power of Thought.

In the early 1800s, a young man in New England, a clockmaker turned healer, made a great metaphysical discovery. "The explanation is the cure," proclaimed Phineas Parkhurst Quimby, and he proceeded to achieve phenomenal success and widespread fame by using techniques that seemed revolutionary at the time. Unbeknownst to him, he had planted the seeds for what was to become the modern New Thought movement. No sooner had the idea been conceived than it emerged through the minds and writings of other great thinkers and philosophers of the day, such as Ralph Waldo Emerson and Henry Thoreau.

A mood for change was sweeping America and, in the fertile soil of inventiveness and spiritual exploration, this philosophy took root and flourished. In England in the late 1800s, Thomas Troward, a retired judge and a man of great knowledge and intellect, gave great impetus to such new ways of thinking. His Edinburgh lectures proved a turning point in many people's lives and were instrumental in inspiring the young Ernest Holmes to study the deeper mysteries of metaphysics. It is ironic, however, that New Thought never really established itself in England, and it was in the United States of America that it really took root and found its home. It is today practised in hundreds of centres, churches and communities from New York to San Francisco, appealing to young and old alike.

Long before the advent of mobile `phones, the Internet and social media, a brave band of ardent pioneers took their message out to the masses. They spoke of a Power for Good in the universe, a God that was available to all regardless of background, and of how we are all worthy of all the good that the universe has to offer. It was a message that ruffled a few feathers and upset a lot of rigid, established ideas, but that nonetheless rapidly gained in popularity. Much of the philosophy of New Thought was gleaned from the Bible and from the teachings of the Master Teacher himself, whose simple stories and parables gave a glimpse of a greater reality. "In my Father's house are many mansions." New Thought enthusiastically embraced the principle of the continuity and eternality of life, ever expanding and moving from one level of consciousness to another.

The movement began essentially as a healing philosophy and produced a number of remarkable healers along the way, although most would say that it is the Spirit within that really does the work. It was a rich and vibrant period when wonderfully gifted teachers emerged whose wisdom and inspired insights changed the course of humanity. Among these was Emma Curtis Hopkins, a mystic of the highest order who was known as 'The teacher of teachers'. She inspired many of the up-and-coming metaphysical leaders of the day, including a very motivated and impassioned young man, Ernest Holmes, himself destined to become a great teacher.

Every Sunday afternoon at four o'clock, a popular radio show was broadcast across the whole of the USA, reaching an audience of millions. The show was called *This Thing Called Life* and Ernest Holmes was its host and presenter. The show always opened with the now familiar statement,

There is a Power for Good in the universe,
greater than you are, and you can use it.

That was in the 1950s when New Thought was flourishing and attracting large and enthusiastic audiences. But the story of the man who conceived the profound spiritual teaching and philosophy we know as Science of Mind dates back to the 1880s.

Ernest Holmes was born on the 27th of January, 1887, the youngest in a family of seven sons. Even at a young age he demonstrated a voracious hunger for knowledge and an enquiring mind that was well ahead of his years. But there was something else, something special and different about Ernest that separated him from his peers. His love of the natural world and a mature understanding of the nature of life marked him out and set him on a course that nobody at the time could possibly have foretold.

New Thought was very much in the ascendancy then and itinerant speakers and healers abounded, demonstrating its principles to thousands of people. The young Ernest was captivated by this new philosophy that talked about God and the power of thought and healing in new ways and he made up his mind to learn as much as possible about the teachings. Perhaps he knew deep down that this was the path he was destined to follow for the rest of his life.

He had great empathy for people, was quick-witted and warm-hearted, and had a natural gift for helping and healing people through the power of prayer. He became a great speaker, travelling the length and breadth of the country riveting audiences with his extraordinary zeal and enthusiasm, extolling the virtues of New Thought in a hugely appealing way. He studied with many of the great metaphysical teachers of the time and, inspired by the knowledge and insights he gained from them together with his own exhaustive study of world religions, Eastern traditions and ancient wisdom, he gradually evolved and refined his own unique ideas and philosophy.

In 1926, Ernest Holmes published the first edition of *Science of Mind*, which became an instant success and attracted a large contingent of enthusiastic disciples. In response to his many followers, the next year he founded the Institute of Religious Science to provide a structured environment for those who wished to become practitioners and teachers in the new movement. This evolved to become the Church of Religious Science, now known as Centers for Spiritual Living, although Ernest had never intended to start a church.

In fact, he gradually retreated from the day to day running of what was to become a substantial organisation, preferring instead to spend his time in quiet contemplation and meditation, writing, healing and speaking. His intention had simply been to create a teaching that was easily accessible, cutting through dogma and doubt and presenting a more positive and joyful version of God, a higher power that was loving, supportive, non-judgmental and available to all.

Intrinsically positive, eternally optimistic and deeply sensitive, he loved people, animals and nature, had an insatiable quest for knowledge and a poetic instinct for the beauty and majesty of life. What strikes one most about the life of this great and gifted man was that he was fun, he enjoyed life and had a great sense of humour; and while he took his work seriously, he did not seem to take himself too seriously. He would often preface his talks with a joke or humorous story to catch the attention of his audience and it was his humanity and warmth that attracted so many people to him.

Whilst I never met the man personally, what I learned from those who did know him was that he was indeed an extraordinary character. Though short in stature, he exerted a massive influence on all who knew him, surrounding himself with positive, success-minded people and believing adamantly that any life condition could be helped and healed by the application of right thought.

It seems that he was a very sociable and popular resident of Hollywood, where he lived in his later years, and where his barbeques, soirées and dinner parties were legendary. His guest list would often include actors, authors and artists as well as prominent scientists and metaphysicians, among them Albert Einstein and the singer Peggy Lee, with whom he was friends. He and his wife Hazel made everyone welcome in their home, which would often buzz with conversation and discussion well into the night. People were intrigued by Ernest Holmes and the stories he would share, and his evenings would often conclude with cosy fireside chats discussing life, God and the universe. He was excited about the possibilities of science and the potential of metaphysics – and the hope that one day the two schools of thought might converge.

He lived a prosperous, full and abundant life, always believed in travelling first class, and was generous, altruistic and magnanimous not only to family, friends and colleagues but to all who came his way. It seems that he not only loved the philosophy but lived the teachings and was a shining example to all who knew him of the principles in action.

It is true that his books are not always easy reading. His writings are profound, deeply analytical, substantially intellectual, often mystical and yet redolent with beautiful poetry and prose. Above all, Ernest Holmes was a man with a vision to change the world for the better and regardless of appearances he remained eternally hopeful and optimistic. It is said that, even in the dark days of World War II, he and countless others continuously prayed for peace and advocated forgiveness and reconciliation.

Holmes' vision of science and spirituality coming together is perhaps edging closer with quantum mechanics' discoveries, for example of interconnectedness and action at a distance ('entanglement'), and a greater acceptance in conventional religion that Heaven is more a state of consciousness than a location. There is a mood for change, a hunger for a new form of spirituality that allows the individual to forge a personal connection with the divine, the power within.

By the late 1950s, Ernest Holmes knew that his work was nearly completed. When his beloved wife Hazel made her transition in 1957, the energy and vitality seemed to drain from him although he had always believed in the continuity of life and the immortality of the soul. Indeed, it had become a core principle of Science of Mind and, in his later years, he became increasingly aware of the presence of Spirit.

"To most of us," he wrote, "immortality means that we shall persist after the experience of physical death, retaining a full recognition of ourselves and having the ability to recognise others. It is not merely pleasing and satisfactory to suppose that we pass from this life to the next in full and complete retention of our faculties – it is logical. I believe in the continuation of the personal life beyond the grave, in the continuity of the individual stream of consciousness with a full recollection of itself and the ability to make itself known. I know that my own experience justifies a complete acceptance in my mind of my own and other people's immortality. I look upon the belief in immortality neither as a vague dream, nor a forlorn hope, but as a proven fact!"

In 1959, at the dedication service for the Whittier Church of Religious Science in California, it is said that he had an extraordinary – some would say mystical – experience. Halfway through his talk, his voice suddenly faltered, the tone of his message noticeably shifted, and it was as if he were being inspired by an altogether higher level of consciousness. Gradually the flow of his words ebbed away, fading into silence.

He paused for a few moments and then in a hushed and almost incredulous tone uttered, "I see it. Oh God... The veil is thin between...I see it... and I shall speak no more."

His work was done and he made his transition on the 9th of April, 1960, leaving a lasting legacy of a teaching, a faith and a profound philosophy that has changed the lives of millions. Science of Mind stands out as teaching that is non-dogmatic, receptive to new ideas and interpretations, and has at its heart a powerful, positive, practical tool for change that can be learned easily and applied effectively to all aspects of life.

In spiritual mind treatment, or affirmative prayer, Ernest Holmes has bequeathed to humanity a unique gift that can transform lives, heal conditions and reconnect us to the God within.

"Spiritual mind treatment', he wrote, "is an affirmation of the divine presence in and through all things, all people and all events. We live in this divine presence and may consciously use the universal law. We must come not only to believe and accept, but also to permanently know that 'there is a power greater than us that we can use.'"

Ernest Holmes was surely one of the most remarkable spiritual teachers and thinkers of the twentieth century. From lowly beginnings to the lofty heights of an organisation that spanned the globe, he created a life-changing philosophy that has heralded a new age of new thinking.

The Science of Mind is the study of life
and the nature of the laws of thought,
the conception that we live in a spiritual universe
and that God is in, through, around and for us.

Spiritual Mind Treatment

A man falls over a cliff and desperately grabs hold of the branch of a tree, hanging precariously on the side of the cliff face. Gradually his grip weakens. The frail branch begins to give way. The man feels himself beginning to fall and cries out in desperation, "Please, God, help me!" From out of the silence, a voice booms in response:

"Let go… Just let go."

The man replies, "Is anybody else there?"

Even in the direst moments, we are not always willing to 'let go and let God', but cling dogmatically to old beliefs and attitudes regardless of the outcome. Truly letting go requires a leap of faith. We must relinquish control and surrender to a higher power, acknowledging that we may not have all the answers and that perhaps there is a higher wisdom and intelligence greater than us that we can call upon in times of need.

Spiritual mind treatment, or affirmative prayer, is all about releasing outmoded beliefs and preconceptions, trusting in that higher intelligence, affirming and giving thanks in advance for the desired outcome even before there may be any outward signs of success.

It is important to note that we are not attempting to solve a problem here, nor achieve any specific result. We are endeavouring to shift our own consciousness into a state of knowing and trust that the perfect possible outcome will be – already is being – achieved. We are clearing any negative or limiting beliefs that may be contrary to our desired goal or purpose and creating a pathway to our highest good. We do not have to limit or specify exactly what that good may look like but be open to infinite possibilities, perhaps even better than expected. By shifting our energy and focus from the problem to the solution, we allow answers to come, ideas to flow, inspiration to be received and healing to take place.

Indeed, when Ernest Holmes first conceived and began using this approach it was with healing in mind and it was offered very much as a form of 'treatment', hence the phrase. But he quickly realised the power and potential of affirmative prayer, not only for treating physical conditions but also in effecting positive changes in people's lives and circumstances. In the early days, it was a simple two-stage process. First and foremost, one recognises and celebrates the omnipresence of Spirit, the divine power and presence in, through and around all things and all people at all times. And secondly one immerses oneself so completely in that consciousness that there is no room for doubt; in that state of aware-ness, faith and certainty, one knows that with God all things are possible.

As Holmes developed his ideas and techniques in order to teach and train others in the art and science of such treatment, the form evolved into the five-step process that has lasted to this day. He would explain that the format was merely a guideline, a blueprint, and that each student should use the words and terminology that resonated best with their own level of understanding. The real power of treatment, he said, did not reside in the words, but in the feeling and intention and the passion behind them, and in there being only one source of power, known as God.

God can only do for us what God can do through us.

In mind treatment we are not beseeching a distant deity to grant our wishes. We are affirming the desired outcome as though it were already accomplished, giving thanks in advance to divine power, and then letting go. We release any attachment to any particular outcome, knowing that our desire or something even better can come to pass and for the highest good of all. There is a magic and a mystery to treatment that transcends doubt, overrides negativity and brings us into the realm of infinite possibilities where miracles can happen.

A heavy rainstorm had just subsided, leaving a translucent shimmer on the pavements, as a sudden beam of sunlight pierced the fast-moving clouds to reveal a stunning, double rainbow. I stopped momentarily to admire the incredible scene, wanting to share it with someone who could appreciate this sudden, uninvited beauty. That same day, during an early morning stroll, I'd had another of those moments of heightened awareness. Russet and gold autumn leaves lay scattered on the pavement when a shaft of sunlight caught the colours of a nearby tree, which seemed to radiate a brilliant amber hue. A tiny grey squirrel dashed across the road and clambered up a tree to seek out nuts for its winter sojourn, while the gleeful singsong of birds perched high up on the branches joyfully announced another day. I reflected on the richness of nature, the miracle of life and the divine presence in all things.

As I write these words, darkness has fallen and the velvet blackness of night is punctuated only by the tiny, distant pinpricks of light from glittering stars perhaps millions of light years away. It is impossible to comprehend the vastness of space, the swirling galaxies and endlessly expanding universe of which we form a minute yet significant part. From the smallest flower to the furthest star there is, however, a divine design and purpose that holds everything together in perfect order and harmony. That same power that keeps the planets in orbit around the

Sun, that controls the spinning of the Earth on its axis and the ebb and flow of the tides, is the same power that flows in, through and around us right now. We call it God, or Spirit, or universal intelligence, or the Source.

This is what spiritual mind treatment is all about – recognising, celebrating and harnessing the one power. When we treat, we are not attempting to change outside conditions or circumstances but seeking to create a shift in our own consciousness and, in the words of Ghandi, to 'become the change we want to see in the world.' As our energy and vibration lift to a higher level, we automatically attract people and circumstances that resonate with this elevated consciousness and, as a consequence, conditions around us begin to change.

The Five-Step Process of Spiritual Mind Treatment

1   We detach from everyday concerns, tune in to Spirit and recognise the Power for Good in the universe that is greater than us.

2   We identify ourselves with this power. We are part of it, it is part of us, we cannot be separate from Spirit. Unified with the creative force of the universe, we become co-creators of our life experience.

3   We identify whatever it is we may wish to manifest in our lives, visualising the desired outcome as if the highest good has already been accomplished.

4   We give thanks in advance for the best possible outcome, trusting that with God anything is possible, even before the first faint signs of change may be apparent.

5   Finally we let go of any doubts or lingering concerns, handing over to that higher power and knowing that whatever happens will be for the highest good. We nurture our aspirations by feeding them with positive thoughts.

But actually there is more, a sixth step we call 'taking inspired action'. Calmly and confidently, without stress, we look out for the clues, the intuitions, unexpected opportunities or divine synchronicities that may come our way. The law of attraction works best when we make the first move, show our intention and commitment, and take action instead of just sitting back waiting for things to happen.

This is what is meant by 'God can only do for us what God can do through us'. We are the channels though which miracles can happen, so we have to play our part. Sometimes our good may come in unexpected ways, through circuitous routes and serendipitous encounters, if we are aware and mindful enough. The job interview or the blind date that did not work out, for example, could lead indirectly to unforeseen blessings and opportunities that simply might not have materialised if we had not 'dared to dream' or taken that first, bold and tentative step into the unknown.

Thus spiritual mind treatment is a perfect expression of faith. And when we gather together with supportive like minds, our faith is strengthened and our treatment invigorated with added energy. 'If we could see a spiritual mind treatment,' wrote Ernest Holmes, 'we would see it as a pathway of light.' Where two or more are gathered, that light is even stronger and the results magnified; when we treat in a group, the effect is multiplied exponentially. We shine a light so bright it may be seen in the Heavens and beyond. In the words of the Master Teacher, we may each 'become the light of the world.'

We are surrounded by a creative and intelligent law
which always tends to bring into our experience
those things that occupy our thought.
Let us imagine that thoughts are things
and that the sum total of all our thinking
decides what happens to us.

Linda has a particular gift for doing treatments as evidenced by the many successful outcomes she has been instrumental in facilitating. She has treated for abundance, for greater wealth in someone's life, for greater happiness, for lost things to be found and of course for healing and wellbeing.

"For me, affirmative prayer is like a magic formula," she says. "I start off by getting into the zone and I do that by using words that evoke a feeling connecting me with what I perceive to be Spirit, a higher power. The words I need just seem to flow through me, then I state what it is I want to realise, what I have in mind. Doing a treatment and repeating positive words, for me, is a very special form of prayer where you are not pleading for anything. It's a positive way of communicating with Spirit. Unlike conventional prayer, here you are stating what it is you want to experience as if it has already happened.

"When I first started learning about treatment it was a five-step process. You had to think about what you were saying at each step. Then suddenly it clicked, a bit like learning to ride a bike and all of a sudden you can ride. You instinctively know to be still, to get yourself into a different state of mind and the words of the prayer take you to another place, to a place of reassurance, of knowing, because you just feel that a weight has been lifted from your shoulders as you release the prayer to Spirit. You know and trust that as your energy changes and you have a shift in consciousness, so your outward experience will change. Something will happen, opportunities will come your way, people will come your way and you will hear or see things that you need to know. It's like a heightened state of awareness for good – and things change.

"I am a creative element in the whole process. I am communicating, and what I am communicating is being heard, is being acted upon because I am corresponding with the cosmos, which is corresponding back to me. And when I speak words of gratitude and love, I can feel a shift within me. And when I release the prayer I feel a burden has been taken from me. I rest assured knowing that because it has happened for me before in my life and for people I've prayed for and been so successful, I know it's going to work.

"I trust that whatever the outcome, it's for the highest good. We've all been taught to come up with the answers to problems, but here we've got a system that says, 'Don't worry about it. The best outcome will come about regardless of what you think, if you truly let go and release it into the law.' The beauty of it is that you are transcending what is going on around you. You are raising your energy way above that, so that you don't have to get involved with the details of the how and the why.

"You can treat for yourself or you can treat for someone else, if they ask you to. And treatment works for all kinds of situations – relationships, say, meeting the right person or resolving difficulties. It can be very effective when there seems to be an impasse and people can't get over a difficult conflict in a relationship. You may say, what if one partner in a relationship doesn't want to be helped? Surely one shouldn't act against their will? Well, as I see it, even in the midst of great conflict there can be light, there can be peace and love because there is the divine. It's like the sun is always shining but it's sometimes obscured by the clouds, so what treatment does is remove the clouds, remove the doubts and the lack of the love.

"If someone is really obstructive, you are still treating for com-passion, love and understanding so there may be a shift in the person you are treating for. And because that person may change, already the relationship between the two people is going to change. After all, you are treating for understanding, you are treating for forgiveness and for compassion. But in the end, no, you cannot treat against someone's will.

"Suppose there's an antagonistic situation at someone's workplace. Ideally, we may like to see harmony achieved and the relationship improved. But the best outcome could be that they shift to another job and that other opportunities start coming their way. And even though the treatment has been done, there can still be follow-ups – as a situation changes so the treatment can change too.

"The essential principle is that the best outcome will always be achieved, whatever is for the highest good. We don't always know the answer but we don't have to evaluate what that outcome will look like because we trust the higher power. We can relax, release and let go.

"People sometimes get frustrated because nothing seems to be happening, they can't see any change. Well, when you plant a seed it doesn't appear to be growing at first and then, all of a sudden, you see a shoot and eventually you see the flower in full bloom. There is always the right and perfect time for things to happen. Or you could think of it like a game of chess – certain pieces have to get into the right positions, synchronicity may have to happen, before you see the endgame. So it doesn't mean the process isn't happening. It may just be around the corner.

"In any case, as they say, 'It is done unto us as we believe.' So, if we believe in the divine, the Power for Good that is omnipresent and omniscient, then in treatment we are seeking to reveal the truth in any situation, to reveal that love and light are at the heart of everything – even if it doesn't seem that way in our experience."

When we truly release and let go with faith,
a weight is lifted off our shoulders and we know,
regardless of appearances,
that the highest possible outcome will be achieved.

"To one who has faith, no explanation is necessary. To one without faith, no explanation is possible," said St Thomas Aquinas. A spiritual concept such as affirmative prayer, however, is not a matter of proof but, ultimately, a journey of faith.

We live in an incredible technological age in which quantum leaps of discovery, innovation and invention are made and the boundaries of what is possible are pushed back year after year. Sometimes, there seems no limit to what Man can achieve. Yet at the furthest limits of our vision and understanding there lies an immaterial yet awesome power and presence that only faith can conceive of – the divine Spirit.

"Faith is the substance of things hoped for," said Ernest Holmes, "the evidence of things unseen."

Faith is the bridge between the known and the unknown, the seen and the unseen. It is the journey that takes us from where we are to where we want to be, the realisation of our dream, the manifestation of our hopes and desires. It is the spark that kindles the fire of our imagination, that transports us out of the ordinary into the extraordinary, the determination to succeed against all the odds.

We are inspired by the wonders of nature, the sun that always shines, the tides that ebb and flow, the changing seasons, the perfect balance of night and day, the infinity of time and space, the mystery of life ever evolving.

But faith takes us further. With faith we reach the crest of the mountain and we move mountains, we see beyond illness and discover the cure, the impossible vision is achieved as we keep going even when the world says, 'Don't bother, give up, go home.' It's the still small voice within that says, 'Yes, we can.'

History bears witness to the many people whose lives have demonstrated the power of faith, from Moses on Mount Sinai and Jesus in Galilee to modern day mystics and inspirational leaders such as Ghandi and Churchill. Even in the darkest hours, when doubt and disappointment threatened to derail their efforts, they never gave up but held firm to their beliefs and inspired millions to achieve the impossible.

"Pure faith," wrote Ernest Holmes, "is spiritual conviction. To have faith, we must have conviction that all is well. To keep faith, we must not allow anything to enter our thought which might weaken its conviction. Faith is built from belief, conviction and trust.

"Spiritual power works through man at the level of his belief... Faith is an affirmative mode of thought. Faith says, 'I can, rather than I cannot.' Whatever we have faith in, we may experience, according to the law of cause and effect. Faith is essential to spiritual mind treatment. Faith is a mental attitude so convinced of its own idea that any contradiction is unthinkable and impossible."

Choices

The waters were rising, barely a house remained intact in the barren landscape. A man was stranded on the roof of his house. He pleaded to God to save him. Then a helicopter flew by, hovered momentarily overhead and lowered a rope to winch the man to safety.

"No thanks," the man cried, "I am waiting for God to save me."

Sometime later a man came by in a rowing boat and offered a hand to pull him to safety. Once again he refused.

"Thanks, but I am waiting for God to rescue me."

Eventually the waters rose further and engulfed the poor man. When in Heaven he met up with God.

"I called you several times," he complained, "but you ignored my pleas for help. Why did you not come to save me?"

"I sent a helicopter to help you," God replied, "but you refused. Then I sent a man in a boat to help you, but once again you said 'No'. How could I help you when you refused to be helped? It was your choice."

We always have a choice. Sometimes the options may not appear crystal clear. It may feel like we are walking through a fog. Then out of the blue may come a flicker of light, an inkling of an idea, a chance meeting or encounter that may open the door to new possibilities. We just need to be willing to stop and listen, to recognise the 'angels in disguise', the intuitive nudges, the sudden inspiration or the people who turn up miraculously out of nowhere. Anything is possible if we are open and receptive to Spirit and to the benevolent flow of life that seeks to support and succour us in times of need.

Several years ago, Linda and I stumbled upon Stansted and Spiritualism and embarked on a path that led us to the Science of Mind and a philosophy that has changed our lives. Sometimes the universe has to shake us before we may heed the signs and head in a new direction. Sometimes the message may come in unexpected invitations, in subtle hints, repeating patterns or even apparent dead ends until we say 'Enough' and hear the message – recognising that we are the masters of our own destiny, the captains of our own ship, the co-creators of our own life experience.

If there is any aspect of our lives we are not happy with, any unresolved issues or challenges, we can remind ourselves that we always have a choice. We can choose to step out of our comfort zone, to change our thinking, beliefs and attitudes, and transmute the nature of our experience so that the patterns of the past need not shape our future. We can step boldly from victimhood ("Why is this happening to me?") to empowerment ("Why is this happening for me?") and learn life lessons along the way.

If we are seeking more meaning, purpose and direction in our lives, if we wish to discover the wisdom and insights that inspired the great minds of history, then we can choose to understand and apply the universal spiritual principles that inspired Ernest Holmes to conceive the Science of Mind teaching, which can create miracles in our lives.

'This has to be a new and wonderful adventure in the art of living. It is going to call for faith, imagination and the will to believe.'

ERNEST HOLMES

There is a story about a mystical squirrel called Jay, who travelled the world in search of the meaning of life. In truth Jay was no ordinary squirrel. Scurrying around collecting nuts and acorns was not enough for him, he wanted more from life. So one fine spring day he bade farewell to his bemused family and friends, packed his bags and set off on an adventure to discover the secret of peace, joy and happiness.

Jay's travels took him to exotic climes and faraway places, to the mountains of Peru and the rainforests of the Amazon. He scaled the highest peaks of the Himalayas and sat in meditation with gurus in Nepal. He stayed in monasteries in Tibet, prayed with the monks and fasted for days on end. He bathed in the warm turquoise waters of Hawaii and conversed with the Huna. He smoked peace pipes with Cherokee Indians and danced with the Shamans. But still he could not find what he was looking for.

He encountered strange, foreign species of squirrels, all shapes and sizes, colours and creeds, brown, black, red and grey. They all seemed happy enough leading their simple squirrel lives. But he wanted more.

Eventually he found himself in the Orient, at the feet of an ancient wise man who told him, "Look within to find God."

It didn't make much sense at the time, so he continued his journey until he arrived at a beautiful white temple in India. Tired from his travels, he welcomed the peace and quiet of the yoga ashram but wondered if he would ever find the secret he was seeking. He spent days in silent meditation and contemplation until a guru drew him aside.

"What you are looking for, you are looking with."

Jay still did not understand and continued wearily on his way. After years of travel and fruitless endeavours, feeling tired, jaded, dejected and disillusioned, he finally headed for home with head held low. When he arrived home, however, he was totally taken aback by the warm, open-hearted reception he received. There was no hint of mockery or ridicule. In fact, groups of squirrels gathered in their dozens to hear the stories of his amazing travels and adventures.

But what struck him most was that everything looked different. He began to see his old world in a new light, as though his eyes had suddenly been opened. The colours seemed sharper, the smells more pungent, and the sensation of the warm sun on his soft fur – and the broad smiles that greeted him – made him realise just how much he had missed being home.

It was as though he were seeing things for the first time. He no longer looked down on the foraging ways of his fellow squirrels but sensed, more than ever, their enthusiasm and glee for the task. He felt an overwhelming sense of compassion for his family and friends who had accepted and welcomed him back without question. He came to realise that what he had been looking for already existed, but that he had not had the eyes to see it. And that the purpose of life, the elusive secret he had sought so long, was all about being happy, being loved and being accepted.

As he sat perched pensively on the top of a tall oak tree, the afternoon sun gleaming gold on the horizon, watching his family and friends scurrying merrily around, he felt a deeply satisfying, all-pervading sense of peace. This was his home. Finally he understood.

News of Jay's remarkable travels and subsequent transformation spread quickly throughout the squirrel kingdom. Squirrels came from far and wide to listen to his wise words and discover the secret of a happy life. He would sit in a peaceful pose before them.

"What you are looking for," he told them, "you are looking with. Be thankful for what you already have. Happiness is an inside job and the meaning of life… well, it's whatever you want it to be."

And with that he would bound off to have fun, to play squirrel games, and to see the good in everyone and everything.

The Sacred Principles

One life, one mind, one power

This chapter describes some of the key principles of spiritual wisdom disseminated through the ages that may serve to guide and inspire us to move from the ordinary to the extraordinary, from stressed to blessed and to become the unique shining lights we are all destined to be.

Everything is energy and energy never dies, it just changes form. We existed before and will continue to exist, evolve and expand, through infinite levels of time, space and consciousness. We are spirit here and now, spiritual beings having a human experience.

There is a divine design, order and purpose behind the universe as there is a divine design, order and purpose to our lives. We are unique, special and significant. We are individualised expressions of the divine, here for a purpose, and part of that purpose is to discover and share our unique gifts and talents with the world.

There is a law of mind, a power of belief and a principle of attraction. We have free will, the power to choose, co-creators of our experience, architects of our own lives. And everything – just everything – begins with a thought.

1   *Thoughts become things*

Every thought we think, every idea born from imagination or inspiration, every creative urge nursed in the cradle of passion and desire, every dream we've ever had, finds its home in universal substance, in the law of mind, in the vast endless energy field of attraction that surrounds us, that permeates every atom and essence of our being and, ultimately, inevitably becomes fashioned and forged into form.

"We are surrounded by a creative and intelligent law, which always tends to bring into our experience those things that occupy our thoughts. Let us imagine that thoughts are things and that the sum total of our thinking decides what happens to us." (Ernest Holmes)

2   *What we focus on expands*

Energy flows where attention goes. What we focus on expands. We need to focus on what we want, not on what we don't want, on the solution, not the problem, on what we have, not on what we lack, on success, not failure. Let us focus on abundance and not on limitation, on peace and not conflict, on health and not illness. For what we focus on will grow and expand and attract more of the same.

3   *It is done to you as you believe*

What we consistently focus on, affirm and believe to be true about ourselves and our lives becomes our experience. Our underlying beliefs and the stories we carry with us from childhood, from our parents, siblings, school, religion and society, determine the way we interpret and perceive our experience and create the filter through which we observe and respond to life.

A belief is simply a habitually repeated thought anchored by strong emotion. We can change our beliefs by changing our thinking. We can change our lives by changing our beliefs. We'll see it when we believe it!

4   The law of attraction

Like attracts like, birds of a feather flock together, what goes around comes around. The law of attraction is constantly at work twenty-four hours a day, seven days a week, and responds to our dominant thoughts and feelings without judgment or discrimination, translating them into our version of reality.

We become what we think about all day long. Our predominant thought patterns tend to manifest as our experience. We are constantly either attracting or repelling our good by the nature of our thoughts, the tone of our words and the depth of our desire.

5   The power of our words

Our words have power. We should choose them wisely, be conscious of their effect both on ourselves and on others. We should complain less, compliment more and be generous with our blessings. A blessing enhances the giver as well as the recipient and touches the observer with a sense of peace and joy. What we send out, comes back to us multiplied. Words can uplift, motivate and inspire or leave us feeling depressed and dejected. So let us choose words that enrich and enliven and kindle a spark of enthusiasm, a feeling of hope and optimism.

"The word you speak today is the law which shall govern your life tomorrow. Today I bless everything I have. I bless everyone around me, I bless the events that transpire in my life, the conditions and situations that surround me. I bless everything that goes out and everything that comes in. I acknowledge an increase of right action in everything I do, say or think. I bless myself and others for we are all partakers of the same divine nature, all living in the one mind, all animated by the same presence, all sustained by the one power." (Ernest Holmes)

6   The power of affirmation

To affirm means to make firm. An affirmation is a statement of belief about ourselves and our life. Affirmations should always be positive, personal and in the present tense. They help to re-programme our subconscious mind to release old negative, limiting belief patterns and replace them with positive, life-affirming thoughts of health, wealth, peace and prosperity.

Everything we think, say and do is to some extent an affirmation. Let us be mindful of affirming what we want and not what we don't want.

"Today I affirm faith in my own affirmations. I know that there is a power flowing through me, taking the form of my belief, acting upon my acceptance, answering my prayer and fulfilling my affirmation. I affirm that every good thing I do will prosper, every person I meet will be blessed, every situation I touch will be helped." (Ernest Holmes)

7   When affirmation does not appear to work

We should think about what we have been thinking or talking about all day long. An affirmation is the beginning of a process, the tip of an iceberg. What matters more is what lies beneath the surface – what we have been thinking, saying and doing all day, all week, which will either reinforce or negate the power of our affirmation. If we are affirming prosperity but talking lack, if we are affirming health but talking illness, if we are affirming for the perfect relationship but privately hankering for our independence and freedom… then it will probably not work.

"The universe corresponds to the nature of your song," says Dr Michael Beckwith. For affirmations really to succeed, our everyday thoughts, words, feelings and actions need to be congruent with and on the same wavelength as what we wish to achieve.

8 The power of 'I am...'

The 'I am…' statement is the most powerful affirmation we can make. When we declare 'I am…' we are virtually claiming the condition, quality or experience as our own. We are making a bold and unequivocal statement to the universe that this is the way we want our life to be. Let's be mindful of what we claim as our own.

We can use positive, empowering statements such as, "I am healthy. I am full of energy. I am happy. I am peaceful and poised. I am abundant and prosperous. I am loving and loved. I am successful in all that I do. I am divinely guided, blessed and inspired at all times."

9 The power of the subconscious mind

The subconscious mind is like a computer. It does not judge or differentiate between fact or fiction, truth or fantasy, but faithfully records everything we think, say and do and recreates it as our reality. We only use a small fraction of our mental capacity in everyday life on a conscious level – about five per cent on average. The rest is subconscious. So let's be mindful of our self-talk, that constant, critical, self-judgmental dialogue we hold with ourselves – and of what others may say to us, even in jest. We should try to avoid negative, limiting tribal beliefs, but feed our subconscious with good news. We can harness the power of our subconscious mind by programming positive thoughts, affirmations and expectations.

10 The power of a new thought

We think thousands of thoughts a day (the National Science Foundation estimates, on average, forty to fifty thousand), many repetitive or routine, many negative. If we want to change our lives, we need to change our thinking and introduce new thought. If we can think happy, healthy, life-affirming thoughts at least fifty-one per cent of the time, we become majority shareholders in our own future well-being.

11 *We cannot deal with a problem at the level of the problem*

"If you always do what you've always done, you'll always get what you've always got," says Antony Robbins. We need to try a different approach, find a new angle, think out the box, take the high ground. We can treat for inspiration, guidance and clarity, and think of problems as simply opportunities in disguise, solutions waiting to happen. Sometimes the most difficult and challenging situations may offer the opportunity for the greatest growth and we may learn lessons and discover blessings and hidden strengths that we never knew existed.

"Change is inevitable, growth is optional," says Harry Morgan Moses.

12 *Visualise a successful outcome as though it has already been accomplished*

Feel the feeling of the wish fulfilled. Fake it until you make it. Act 'as if'. We can make a space, prepare a place for the person, thing or situation we wish to attract or manifest into our life. This sends a signal to the universe that we are ready, willing, worthy and available to receive our good. Anticipate success, expect the best and make it happen.

13 *Take a moment*

Detach, take a breath, take a moment. We should give ourselves time to consider our responses, and the consequence of our actions, before reacting perhaps rashly and impulsively in the heat of the moment. Whatever seems so urgent and important right now may fade into insignificance in an hour's, a day's or a week's time, if we stand back, see the bigger picture, put things in context and keep our peace and poise intact.

14 *The power of forgiveness*

Forgiveness is the greatest gift we can give ourselves. Forgiveness is freedom, it is healing. Forgiveness is not about condoning inappropriate behaviour or making the other person right; it is about letting go and releasing any negative thoughts, feelings or energy that may be harming us, more than anyone else, and holding us back from experiencing our greater good. And saying 'Sorry' can pour soothing balm on a difficult situation and place us on the higher ground.

"Sometimes it is better to be kind than to be right," said Dr Wayne Dyer.

"How often do we condemn when we should forgive, how often censure when we might praise? What untold grief of heart may be relieved by words of cheer and forgiveness?" (Ernest Holmes)

"Forgiveness is the fragrance that the violet sheds on the heel that has crushed it," said Mark Twain.

15 The power of detachment

A Zen master instructed his student to muster all the vitriolic abuse he could and hurl it directly it at him. The student was perplexed but did what he was told, ranting and raving for hours until he was completely exhausted. During this time, the Zen master remained perfectly calm and undisturbed.

"How can you remain so calm," demanded the now angry student, "when I am hurling such abuse at you?"

"Well," replied the master, "if someone offers you a gift and you refuse to accept it, who does it belong to?"

16 The power of gratitude

Being grateful for what we already have attracts more things to be grateful for. We attract what we think about, and thank about, all day long. By saying 'Thank you' for a gift, a compliment or a blessing, we are participating in the law of circulation, completing a cycle of energy. Giving and receiving are two sides of the same coin. By being grateful and focusing on the blessings in our lives – as opposed to what we don't have, don't like, or don't want – we create an atmosphere of attraction, an environment more conducive to success, healing and contentment.

"If the only prayer we will ever say in our entire life is 'Thank you', it will be enough," said Meister Eckhart.

"The mental attitude of gratitude draws the mind into closer touch with the Source from which the blessings come," said Wallace Wattles.

17 Perception is projection

As within, so without. As above, so below. The outer world is a reflection of our inner thoughts and feelings. What we notice, compliment or criticise in other people is often a reflection of what we love most – or like least – about ourselves. We can only recognise a quality in someone else if the essence or potential of that characteristic already resides in us. If we change our point of view and perspective, we may begin to notice more blessings and opportunities for growth in every situation. We may move away from, 'Why has this happened to me?' to 'Why has this happened for me?' – from victimhood to empowerment.

18 The point of power is always in the present moment

The past is history, the future a mystery, all we have is the gift of now, which is why we call it the present. We cannot change the past but we can change the way we think about it. Everything that has happened to us in the past has contributed to who and what we are right now. But we can change our future by what we think, say and do today. Our thoughts, feelings, attitude and actions today are constantly creating our tomorrows. What we think about, we bring about, one step, one thought, one day at a time.

19 The ripple effect

Karma, consequence, the law of cause and effect… every action creates a reaction or consequence. What we send out comes back to us one way or another. What goes around comes around. We need to be mindful of the choices we make, the actions we take and the ripples they create on the surface of time.

20 Optimist or pessimist?

Who sees the world as it really is, the optimist or the pessimist? The answer is both, because it all depends what we focus on. Both will find the evidence to support their case.

"An optimist sees an opportunity in every problem," said Winston Churchill. "A pessimist sees a problem in every opportunity."

21 Upgrade the positive, downgrade the negative

Life is very much what we make it. We can see the glass as half empty or half full. We can choose to accentuate the positive and downgrade the negative, become the bearer of good tidings rather than a messenger of doom. If there's good news, let's make it fabulous, magnificent, incredible, breathtaking. If it's not such good news, let's not give it too much energy, focus and attention, but put it on the back page. Even keep it to oneself.

'If you have nothing nice to say, better say nothing at all.'

There is a lot of good going on in the world that goes unnoticed and unannounced in favour of the dramas and disasters that hit the headlines. We can create our own headlines, put a smile on people's faces and bring a little sunshine into somebody's life.

22 The power of intention

What we give our attention to, we energise. But what we give our intention to, we actualise. Intention is the driving force, the dynamic that translates ideas, dreams and desires into reality. There is an irresistible force behind intention that transcends doubt, overcomes uncertainty and creates an inevitable pathway to success. When we set a goal, we plant a potential. When we set an intention, we commit to action.

23 The questions we ask determine the answers we get

If we don't like the answers we are getting, perhaps we should change the questions we are asking. Instead of asking, 'Why do I feel so tired?' we could ask, 'How can I have more energy?' Instead of wondering, 'Why do my relationships never seem to work out?' we could ask, 'How can I have more satisfying, enjoyable and long-lasting relationships?'

Energy flows where attention goes.

"The universe corresponds to the nature of your song," says Michael Beckwith. "Sing a different tune."

24 The power of mindfulness

There's a practice called PMA: present moment awareness. It means being in the now, keeping centred, keeping focused with our eye on the ball. We need to take time to smell the roses, admire a rainbow, enjoy the silence or just be in the presence of beauty and peace. And take life one moment, one day at a time.

25 Be the change you want to see in the world

We cannot change other people, we can only change ourselves. By so doing we send out ripples of positive energy that may touch and affect the people around us and, in due course, change the world.

26 The power of a group

'Where two or more are gathered…' There is a powerful energy when groups of like-minded people come together in common purpose and intention. We should share our goals, hopes and dreams with people who understand and will support us. Never underestimate the power of a group.

"There is a law of good," wrote Ernest Holmes, "a power in the universe greater than us, and we can use it. It will multiply a thousand times through the united consciousness of a group."

27 Go for gold

Let's think big, aim high, be the best we can be. Let us take inspired action and move inexorably in the direction of our dreams, unconcerned with the outcome, relaxed and letting go, giving thanks in advance.

"Nothing is too good to be true," wrote Florence Schinn. "Nothing is too wonderful, nothing is too good to last, when you look to God for your good."

28 The power of letting go

When we let go of attachment to an outcome – and stop trying to manage, manipulate or control the result – magical things happen. As we release any resistance or anxiety, events and circumstances orchestrate the best possible solution. Surrendering to the path of least resistance does not mean giving up or giving in, but allows the flow of a higher power, a wisdom greater than we are to work for our highest good.

29 Nothing has any meaning other than what we give it

Once we stop labelling experiences as either good or bad, we open up to the flow of infinite possibilities. Sometimes from so-called disasters important lessons and untold blessings may be gleaned. If we can just be open and receptive to the Power for Good, untainted by judgment and preconceptions, we may truly become in tune with the infinite.

30 The one power

We have at our disposal an awesome power, a power that created the universe, our Sun and Moon and stars, that keeps the planets in perfect balance, order and harmony, that controls the ebb and flow of the tides, the motion of the oceans, the ceaseless rhythm of the seasons, that flows through aeons of time and eternity and expresses itself through the inventiveness of Man from the very beginnings of time to the modern science that sits at the dawn of the future.

Some call it God, or infinite intelligence, the divine mind or the one power. It is within us and around us. It courses through the veins of the universe. It is the heartbeat at the centre of life. It is the power of creative thought.

31 The game of life

Many people believe that life happens 'to us', that we have no say in proceedings. But the truth is we are not victims or passive observers, but active participants in 'the game of life'.

"Most people consider life a battle," wrote Florence Schinn, "but it is not a battle, it is a game. It is a game however, which cannot be played successfully without the knowledge of spiritual law."

We live, move and have our being in a universe of love and law. The law shows us the way, but it is the love that lightens the path and reveals the true essence and quality of what we call God.

'Science of Mind is the study of life and the nature of the laws of thought, the conception that we live in a spiritual universe and that God is in, through, around and for us.'

ERNEST HOLMES

Postscript

Writing this book has been a labour of love, a remarkable journey in itself, revisiting some of the landmark events and experiences that have shaped my life and formed the foundation of my spiritual philosophy and outlook. It is my hope and desire that my experiences may inspire you the reader to embark upon your own journey of discovery, to take the next step, to delve deeper and experience for yourself the magic, mystery and miracle of the Power for Good in the universe that is greater that we are – and use it for yourself and for the benefit of others.

'Your life is God's gift to you.
What you do with it is your gift to God.'

Eric Butterworth

Recommended Reading & Viewing

Shortcut to a Miracle	Michael & Elizabeth Rann Arrott
The Secret (book & DVD)	Rhonda Byrne
The Key to Living the Law of Attraction	Jack Canfield
The Seven Spiritual Laws	Deepak Chopra
Ordering from the Cosmic Kitchen	Patricia Crane
The Shift (from Ambition to Meaning) (DVD)	Dr Wayne Dyer
The Four Spiritual Laws of Prosperity	Edwene Gaines
You Can Heal Your Life	Louise Hay
Louise Hay the Movie (DVD)	Louise Hay
The Power of the Subconscious Mind	Dr Joseph Murphy
The Power of Positive Thinking	Norman Vincent Peale
Adventures of the Soul	James Van Praagh
The Game of Life (anthology)	Florence Scovel Schinn
Highway to Healing	David Serlin
Shine On – Purposeful Poems	Linda Serlin

If you have enjoyed this book...

Local Legend is committed to publishing the very best spiritual writing, both fiction and non-fiction. You might also enjoy:

A UNIVERSAL GUIDE TO HAPPINESS
Joanne Gregory (ISBN 978-1-910027-06-6)

Joanne is an internationally acclaimed clairaudient medium with a celebrity contact list. Growing up, she ignored her evident psychic abilities, fearful of standing out from others, and even later, despite witnessing miracles daily, her life was difficult. But then she began to learn the difference between the psychic and the spiritual, and her life turned round.

This is her spiritual reference handbook – a guide to living happily and successfully in harmony with the energy that created our universe. It is the knowledge and wisdom distilled from a lifetime's experience of working with Spirit.

THE QUIRKY MEDIUM
Alison Wynne-Ryder (ISBN 978-1-907203-47-3)

Alison is the co-host of the TV show *Rescue Mediums*, in which she puts herself in real danger to free homes of lost and often malicious spirits. Yet she is a most reluctant medium, afraid of ghosts! This is her amazing and often very funny autobiography, taking us backstage of the television production as well as describing how she came to discover the psychic gifts that have brought her an international following.

Winner of the Silver Medal in the national Wishing Shelf Book Awards.

A MESSAGE FROM SOURCE

Grace Gabriella Puskas (ISBN 978-1-910027-00-4)

Beautiful and inspiring poetry of the Spirit that reaches deep within the consciousness, awakening the reader to higher states of awareness, spiritual connection and love. The author, in familiar and thoughtful language, explores the power of meditation, the nature of the universe and of time, our place within the environment and who we truly are as creative beings of light and sound.

Winner of our national Spiritual Writing Competition.

AURA CHILD

A I Kaymen (ISBN 978-1-907203-71-8)

One of the most astonishing books ever written, telling the true story of a genuine Indigo child. Genevieve grew up in a normal London family but from an early age realised that she had very special spiritual and psychic gifts. She saw the energy fields around living things, read people's thoughts and even found herself slipping through time, able to converse with the spirits of those who had lived in her neighbourhood. This is an uplifting and inspiring book for what it tells us about the nature of our minds.

REDEEMING LUCIFER

Lennart Svensson (ISBN 978-1-910027-20-2)

This extraordinary novel is a tale in the finest tradition of legendary deeds, a blend of esotericism, pure imagination and acutely observed historical fact. A Russian army captain and his trusted striker find themselves journeying through parallel, mystical worlds in an epic quest to find Lucifer, no less, and to heal the world of its ills. But first, an ultimate, cosmic battle must be fought… This book challenges each of us to examine our life's purpose. Lennart Svensson is a Swedish academic and this is his debut novel in English.

THE HOUSE OF BEING

Peter Walker (ISBN 978-1-910027-26-4)

Acutely observed verse by a master of his craft, showing us the mind, the body and the soul of what it is to be human in this glorious natural world. A linguist and a priest, the author takes us deep within the surface of life and writes with sensitivity, compassion and, often, with searing wit and self-deprecation. This is a collection the reader will return to again and again.

A winner of our national Spiritual Writing Competition.

These titles are available as paperbacks and eBooks.
Further details and extracts of these and many
other beautiful books may be seen at
www.local-legend.co.uk

Lightning Source UK Ltd.
Milton Keynes UK
UKHW020619310120
357947UK00016B/1255